OMBAT AIRCRAFT

118 He 162 *VOLKSJÄGER* UNITS

SERIES EDITOR TONY HOLMES

118

COMBAT AIRCRAFT

Robert Forsyth

He 162 *VOLKSJÄGER* UNITS

OSPREY
PUBLISHING

First published in Great Britain in 2016 by Osprey Publishing
Kemp House, Chawley Park, Cumnor Hill, Oxford OX2 9PH, UK
1385 Broadway, 5th Floor, New York, NY 10018, USA

29 Earlsfort Terrace, Dublin 2, Ireland

Osprey Publishing, part of Bloomsbury Publishing Plc

© 2016 Osprey Publishing – Email: info@ospreypublishing.com

A CIP catalogue record for this book is available from the British Library.

ISBN: 978 1 4728 1457 9
PDF eBook ISBN: 978 1 4728 1458 6
ePub eBook ISBN: 978 1 4728 1459 3

Edited by Tony Holmes
Cover artwork by Mark Postlethwaite
Aircraft profiles by Jim Laurier
Index by Angela Hall
Originated by PDQ Digital Media Solutions, UK
Printed and bound in India by Replika Press Private Ltd.

21 22 23 24 25   10 9 8 7 6 5 4 3

Osprey Publishing supports the Woodland Trust, the UK's leading woodland
conservation charity. Between 2014 and 2018 our donations were spent on their
Centenary Woods project in the UK.

www.ospreypublishing.com

Acknowledgements
My thanks to those who have contributed help and information on the He 162
over the years, namely Eric Mombeek, Eddie J Creek, J Richard Smith,
Nick Beale, Steve Coates, Ted Oliver and Chris Thomas.

Front Cover
On the clear and bright morning of 4 May 1945, just a few hours before the German surrender in western Europe, Leutnant Rudolf Schmitt, the *Staffelkapitän* of 1./JG 1, took off from Leck airfield in northern Germany in He 162 'White 1' to search for enemy fighters that had reportedly been seen in the near vicinity. During his flight, Schmitt observed what he identified as a Hawker Tempest southeast of Husum and opened fire. He recorded in his logbook that he had 'fired upon the enemy aircraft with effect'. The low-level encounter was over in seconds, but it had been a rare meeting between the He 162 *Volksjäger* and an RAF fighter in the closing hours of the war.

Although he subsequently claimed a Tempest destroyed, Schmitt was not credited with the kill. Whilst it remains improbable that he actually shot an enemy aircraft down, Schmitt cannot be denied the likelihood that he opened fire 'with effect' on a single-engined fighter or fighter-bomber and assumed he had damaged it, perhaps even sufficiently to cause it to go down.

Mark Postlethwaite's cover painting depicts the encounter over the fields of Schleswig-Holstein in what must have been one of the last such instances during the war in Europe

CONTENTS

CHAPTER ONE

THE PEOPLE'S FIGHTER

As Allied forces drove ever deeper into Nazi Germany in 1945, so their progress yielded many astounding discoveries. By the end of the first week of May, as World War 2 in northwest Europe drew to a close, the British Second Army's VIII Corps had fought its way from the river Rhine, across northwest Germany to finally push north into the flat, open farmland of Schleswig-Holstein. Its light armoured units reached Kiel and then crossed the Kiel Canal, heading for the Danish border. Along the path of their advance, aside from some bitter fighting, elements of the Corps and their associated units had discovered the horrors of the Bergen-Belsen concentration camp and numerous other testimonies to the brutality of the Nazi regime.

It was almost at the 'end of the road', however, on 6 May that VIII Corps came across another astonishing find. That day, its vehicles reached the small town of Leck, 30 km west of Flensburg and just south of the Danish border. On the northern edge of the town was an airfield, and it was here that a considerable number of Luftwaffe aircraft had assembled, ready for the inevitable surrender and the arrival of Allied forces. As the British tanks rumbled over the airfield perimeter, there came into sight 22 distinctive and diminutive aircraft lined up in two impressive and closely ranked rows on either side of one of the taxi tracks. Distinctive because these aircraft were void of propellers and, uniquely, their power units were carried atop their fuselages, behind which was a twin tail arrangement.

The accomplished design partnership of Professor Ernst Heinkel (right) and his Senior Design Engineer, Siegfried Günter, was responsible for the production of many renowned aircraft, including the He 111 that Heinkel is referring to on the drawing board in this photograph. The two men would be involved in the commissioning of the He 162 from the outset

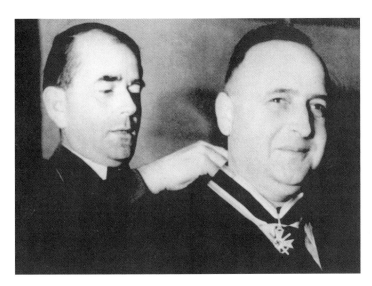

Hauptdienstleiter Dipl-Ing Karl-Otto Saur (right) is presented with the Knight's Cross of the War Service Cross with Swords by the German Armaments Minister, Albert Speer. The energetic and blunt engineer was the early driving force behind the *Volksjäger* project

The men of VIII Corps had stumbled across the only operationally ready unit of Heinkel He 162s. These were the Luftwaffe's last examples of mass-produced, jet-powered technology, and a paradox in design – rushed and cheap (at least compared to the other German jets, the Messerschmitt Me 262 and the Arado Ar 234), but supposedly quick and easy to build, easy to fly and fast. This was the *Volksjäger* (the 'People's Fighter'), a final attempt to overcome the Allied bomber threat with a machine available in significant numbers, which could be flown by relatively inexperienced pilots and yet be able to outperform any fighter the enemy had. Yet, understandably, this was seen by many in Germany as an unrealistic and unattainable goal.

The *Volksjäger* concept originated with civil engineer and committed Nazi Hauptdienstleiter Dipl-Ing Karl-Otto Saur, who Hitler once described as being the 'genius in our armaments industry'. By the summer of 1944 Saur believed that the Luftwaffe fighter arm was a spent force, no longer able to conduct effective operations against the Allies. As such, a radical alternative was needed, and Saur issued a proposal for a small, cheap, high-performance jet fighter that could be mass-produced under what he termed as 'forced action'. According to the erstwhile General of the Fighter Arm, Generalleutnant Adolf Galland, 'Saur gave Göring the idea which he jumped at immediately – as he did to all proposals that were out of the ordinary and sufficiently crazy.'

Saur's idea also won support from Generaloberst Alfred Keller, the head of the *Nationalsozialistisches Fliegerkorps* (NSFK), the Nazi Party-controlled, flying training and sports association, whose auxiliary branch, the *Flieger Hitler-Jugend* (Flying Hitler Youth), offered aircraft model-building courses and glider flying to boys of school age. Keller believed that with the right type of aircraft, and following a limited period of glider tuition, boys as young as 15 to 17 years of age could be quickly trained to fly combat missions. Keller reasoned that if the simple but reliable new *Volkswagen* (People's Car) could be driven by virtually anyone with the minimum of instruction, then why not the same for an aircraft? Galland recalled;

'Good old Keller, whom we called the "Father of Heroes", was won over by this. One day he came to see me in order to discuss the preparations. He intended tackling the problem without any technical knowledge, merely aided by his NSFK *Standartenführer* and *Gruppenführer*. He thought he had found a new way of justifying the existence of his *Korps*. However, I dissuaded him after a few days.'

But by this stage the idea had already reached Reichsmarschall Hermann Göring, who was becoming increasingly desperate to find a way to appease

Hitler. The *Führer* was impatient and scornful over the Luftwaffe's failure to hit back at the Allied air forces that were operating with increasing impunity over the Reich. Thus, at this dark time in the war, Göring seized upon the idea, envisaging whole units of fanatical, NSFK-trained *Hitler-Jugend* engaging the enemy's bomber formations with a new resolve. By drawing on such a vast, untapped well of manpower, the rate of supply of pilots would be equal to the number of aircraft that Saur confidently projected would roll off the assembly lines set up in underground and strategically distant factories using round-the-clock production.

The man who took the *Volksjäger* idea to initial development was Oberst Siegfried Knemeyer, the head of flight development in the Technical Equipment Office of the Reichsluftministerium (RLM). Before the war Knemeyer had worked on the development of instrument flying and had

Oberst Siegfried Knemeyer, an extremely experienced pilot and technician, is seen here during an inspection of the Horten H IIIe tailless glider. In 1944, while working for the RLM Technical Office, he oversaw the early development of the *Volksjäger*, envisaging a fighter able to take off from short runways and with a single jet engine mounted above the wing

qualified as an engineer. He became a skilled pilot, and with his considerable knowledge of electronics, he later undertook test flights and operational missions in many different aircraft over Europe and North Africa. In April 1943 he was appointed Technical Officer to the *Angriffsführer England*, the command responsible for bombing raids against the British Isles, and was then assigned to Göring's personal staff, where he encouraged development of the Me 262.

However, Knemeyer was astute enough to recognise that although the Me 262 provided the Luftwaffe with a first-rate interceptor, the aircraft lacked performance at low altitude, which was where enemy fighters were now becoming an increasing threat as they attacked Luftwaffe airfields and strafed supply trains and troops on the ground. Nor did Knemeyer believe that the existing piston-engined Bf 109 and Fw 190 compensated in this regard. As he wrote shortly after the war;

'It became absolutely essential to develop a high-speed, single-seater fighter that had a sufficiently good performance which would enable it to take off when enemy aircraft were actually sighted. In addition, due to the bombing of our large airfields with long runways, these new fighters had to be able to take off in a very short distance and thus enable small landing grounds to be used. The mass production of such an aircraft had to be on such a scale as would enable the enemy to be engaged at any point and during the entire duration of their flight.

'By limiting the endurance and the armament requirement for this new aircraft, the existing jet fighter [the Me 262] would have fulfilled the requirements. However, this aircraft had to be ruled out since it was not possible to produce the numbers that would have been required for combating these low-flying attacks and, in particular, because the provision of two power units per airframe was quite beyond the capacity of industry.'

Knemeyer opined that this new, low-altitude interceptor would need to be capable of making an unassisted takeoff in less than 600 metres, and of achieving high speed at low and medium altitudes, with a minimum speed of 750 km/h at sea level. In terms of manufacture, the introduction of such an aircraft would cause minimal disruption to the existing Me 262 and Ar 234 production programmes and would use wood as a primary material, drawing on the skills of furniture manufacturers and similar suppliers. This plan would be aided by the cancellation of other aircraft such as the all-wood Ta 154 fighter.

Crucially, the new aircraft would also use just one jet engine, and since production of the Jumo 004 was already at maximum output, it was planned to adopt the BMW 003. The problem was that although the BMW 003 was the engine that German aircraft manufacturers were waiting for, its development had been dogged by endless problems associated with turbine failures, mainly due to fatigue in welded joints and heat-induced brittleness in the turbine blades. In July 1944 work on a first batch of 100 BMW 003s at a dedicated company flight-test centre at Oranienburg was still ongoing. Nevertheless, Knemeyer further proposed that the single engine should be mounted above the wing, which, despite a loss in longitudinal stability, would offer a corresponding decrease in the risk of fire.

This was not a new concept to German aircraft designers. In February 1943, the Henschel Flugzeugwerke produced a design known as the Hs 132, a small, high-speed, mid-wing, anti-shipping aircraft with twin tail fins and a single turbojet mounted above its metal fuselage. The wings were to be made of wood with a plywood skin, and the pilot was to lie prone behind a glazed nose so as to be able to withstand forces of up to 10g. This way, the Hs 132 could attack the ships of the anticipated Allied invasion fleet in a shallow dive, reaching speeds of up to 910 km/h. The finished design bore a striking resemblance to the aircraft that would eventually emerge as the Heinkel He 162, but Henschel progressed only as far as building a wind-tunnel model and the fuselage and wings of the first prototype.

Meanwhile, Knemeyer's outline requirements formed the basis of an RLM specification issued in July 1944 that called for a jet aircraft to be completed in the unprecedented time of eight weeks, with a mock-up to be ready by 1 October. It was further decreed that a prototype should be ready to fly by 1 December, with series production commencing from 1 January 1945. However, from this point until early September 1944, further planning on the idea of a *Volksjäger* seems to have stopped.

Then, during the evening of 7 September, a top-priority teleprint message arrived at the Project Office of the Ernst Heinkel Aktiengesellschaft (EHAG) at Schwechat, in Vienna, addressed to Professor Ernst Heinkel, his Senior Design Engineer, Siegfried Günter and another engineer, Ing Heinz Meschkat. The message had come from the firm's Oranienburg works, north of Berlin, and may well have been sent unofficially by Dipl-Ing Karl Frydag, Heinkel's RLM-assigned Generaldirektor (General Manager). In addition to his position with Heinkel, Frydag acted as Technical Director of the Henschel Flugzeugwerke and, somewhat fortuitously, he was also leader of the influential Main Committee for Aircraft Construction in the Armaments Ministry, and thus a close associate of Saur, with whom he had regular discussions on aircraft production.

The message from Oranienburg contained a still-unreleased detailed tender specification from the RLM for a jet fighter that was due to be sent

Dipl-Ing Karl Frydag, the General Manager at EHAG, was an *éminence grise* behind the *Volksjäger* project. His holding of several positions simultaneous to that of his role with Heinkel gave him insight and influence, as did his close association with Karl-Otto Saur, and he orchestrated events in EHAG's favour

shortly to Heinkel (officially), Arado, Blohm und Voss, Fieseler, Focke-Wulf, Messerschmitt, Junkers and Siebel. The tender called for a fighter to be built from existing components and powered by a BMW 003 engine. It was eventually released the next day by Oberst Ulrich Diesing, the Head of Air Technical Equipment at the RLM, under the title '*Volksjäger*'.

At Schwechat on the 9th, Ernst Heinkel and his team moved quickly, fully exploiting the advantages in time and knowledge they had over their competitors. Heinkel ordered his engineers to re-examine a project specification he had issued the previous July known as the P 1073. This was for a *Schneller Strahljäger* (High-Speed Jet Fighter) to be powered by two HeS 011 or Jumo 004C turbojets. The P 1073 was planned as a potential replacement for the Me 262, but possessing a much higher critical Mach number in the order of 0.94 and an increase in speed of at least 70 km/h. Most of the initial studies featured a 35-degree swept-back wing and a V-type tailplane, with two staggered HeS 011 engines mounted dorsally and ventrally on the fuselage, but later plans would include single-engined proposals. The HeS 011 would give a maximum speed of 1010 km/h at 6000 m.

However, due to the non-availability of this engine, for the immediate future at least, it was proposed to use Jumo 004C engines, which would offer a maximum speed of 940 km/h at 6000 m. Flight endurance at full power was one hour at 11,000 m, while climbing time to the same height was ten minutes, with a range of 1000 km. In order to accommodate a nosewheel, the ventrally mounted engine would be offset to the right. For the same reason, the proposed MK 103 30 mm cannon was to be fitted asymmetrically, with two MG 151/20 20 mm cannon installed on either side of the fuselage.

To conform to the *Volksjäger* tender, Heinkel scaled down the P 1073 to a size that would work with the less powerful BMW 003 and redrew the design as the P 1073-15 with straight wings and twin tail fins.

By the time Diesing's 'Very Urgent' tender message arrived at the offices of the other aircraft companies, Heinkel had enjoyed a two-day lead. Dutifully, however, each firm assessed the RLM request. The requirement called for a fighter with a maximum speed of 750 km/h at sea level, a takeoff distance of not more than 500 m, the ability to operate from poor airfields and an endurance of at least 30 minutes at sea level at 100 per cent thrust. The aircraft was to incorporate an armament of two MK 108 30 mm cannon with 80-100 rounds per gun, or alternatively two MG 151/20 20 mm cannon with 200-250 rounds per gun, and be equipped with instrumentation and basic FuG 15 or FuG 16 VHF radio transceiver equipment for fair weather operations only.

As far as was practical, wood and steel were to be employed in the construction, although armour plating was to be incorporated to allow adequate defence for the pilot and the aircraft's 30 mm ammunition against a frontal attack with 13 mm ammunition. The fuel tanks were to also be armour-plated, but the manufacturers were asked to investigate whether the takeoff run could be reduced if the ammunition load and weight of armour plating were reduced. Perhaps the most demanding stipulation was that the competing proposals should be ready for examination by the RLM's Fighter Aircraft Development Group within three to five days! However,

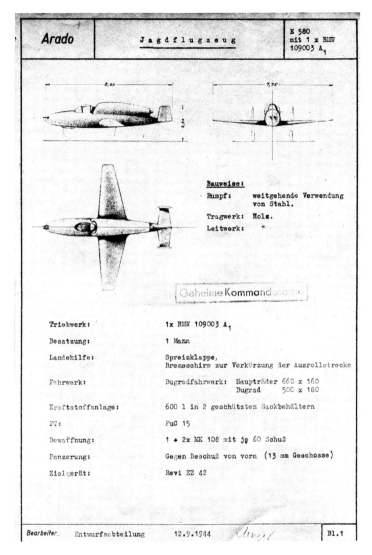

Arado	Jagdflugzeug	E 580 mit 1 x BMW 109003 A₁

Bauweise:
Rumpf: weitgehende Verwendung von Stahl.
Tragwerk: Holz.
Leitwerk: "

Geheime Kommandosache

Triebwerk:	1x BMW 109003 A₁
Besatzung:	1 Mann
Landehilfe:	Spreizklappe, Bremsschirm zur Verkürzung der Ausrollstrecke
Fahrwerk:	Bugradfahrwerk: Haupträder 660 x 160 Bugrad 500 x 180
Kraftstoffanlage:	600 l in 2 geschützten Sackbehältern
FT:	FuG 15
Bewaffnung:	1 + 2x MK 108 mit je 60 Schuß
Panzerung:	Gegen Beschuß von vorn (13 mm Geschosse)
Zielgerät:	Revi EZ 42

Bearbeiter.	Entwurfsabteilung	12.9.1944		Bl.1

The Arado E 580 was one of the submissions for the *Volksjäger* contract. A small, unswept, low-wing aircraft, it was to incorporate a BMW 003 engine, two 30 mm MK 108 cannon and an EZ 42 gunsight, but it was rejected by the RLM

on 12 September, *Oberkommando der Luftwaffe* (OKL) confirmed by telegram that this deadline had been extended to the 14th.

Arado, Blohm und Voss, Focke-Wulf, Heinkel and Junkers picked up the chalice and went to work, each company submitting at least one design, with Focke-Wulf supplying two. Fieseler and Siebel were unable to comply with the specification, while Messerschmitt declined to tender. Indeed, Professor Willy Messerschmitt would later scribe a vitriolic note on the *Volksjäger* plan in which he damned the whole idea as delusional and a failure.

Arado based its resulting E 580 *Volksjäger* proposal on a design dating from 1943 to produce a small, unswept, low-wing aircraft with a wingspan of 7.75 m, a length of 8 m and a wing surface of 10 square metres. Unusually, the intake of the BMW 003 was partially obscured by the cockpit canopy. The E 580 incorporated a tricycle undercarriage with wide-track mainwheels and was to carry two 30 mm MK 108 cannon, but it did not appear to include two 20 mm MG 151/20 cannon as per the RLM request. In this configuration, the aircraft would weigh 2635 kg and possess a top speed of 750 km/h, with a rate of climb of 17 metres per second at ground level and four metres per second at 9800 m. It would be able to take off within 570 m and had a range of 610 km, with an endurance of 22 minutes. The Arado design was ready for submission on 12 September 1944.

Blohm und Voss submitted the P 211.02 'Einstrahltriebkleinstjäger' (single-jet-propelled mini-fighter), which was based on an earlier design known as the P 211.01 featuring swept-back wings fitted to a tubular steel spar from which a BMW 003 engine would be suspended. Designed by Dr-Ing Richard Vogt, the P 211.02 was to be built from a mix of 50 per cent steel, 23 per cent wood, only 13 per cent Duralumin (which was in short supply in Germany by mid-1944) and six per cent miscellaneous materials. The 8.08 m-long, 7.6 m-span, high-wing aircraft had a pod and boom fuselage in which the pilot was housed above the turbojet intake duct that gave stability to the nose section and from which extended a retractable tricycle undercarriage. The engine exhausted below the boom, which also served as a fuel tank, and tail. Weighing 3100 kg, the P 211's maximum speed was forecast at 767 km/h, with a rate of climb of 14.05 metres per second at ground level and 2.46 metres per second at 9000 m and a range of 720 km. The aircraft would be able to take off in 650 m if on a concrete runway and in 800 m if on grass, and it would be armed with two MK 108 30 mm cannon.

Like Heinkel, Focke-Wulf submitted a scaled-down version of an earlier project from April 1943, the twin-boom Fw 226 *Flitzer* ('Streaker') that incorporated both a jet engine – originally the HeS 011 – as well as an option for rocket power. By September 1944 the design could be reworked as a jet fighter, with rocket power boost for quick, high-altitude interception work; as a jet fighter with additional rocket boost for climb to medium altitudes; or as a jet-powered fighter only, without rocket assistance but with two hours flying time at 10,000 m. The aircraft would carry either two MK 108 30 mm cannon in the forward fuselage beneath the cockpit or two MK 108 cannon in the fuselage and two MG 151 20 mm cannon in the wings, with provision for a ZFR telescopic gunsight. In the former configuration, the loaded weight of the *Flitzer* with 830 kg of fuel would be 3660 kg, while in the latter configuration it would be 4350 kg, with 1250 kg of fuel.

By simply substituting the HeS 011 for a BMW 003 and removing the rocket power, Focke-Wulf created the mid-wing '*Volksflitzer*'. Armament was to consist of two MK 108s, and all-up flight weight would have been 3000 kg, while endurance would have been approximately 50 minutes at 10,000 m. A more serious proposal was the Focke-Wulf '*Volksflugzeug*', which featured a long intake duct for a BMW 003 with either a high swept or unswept wing with a span of 7.5 m and a distinctive swept-back tailplane mounted on top of the tail fin. Measuring 8.80 m in length and weighing 3050 kg, the *Volksflugzeug* would have needed a 1000 m takeoff run and would have climbed at 14.5 metres per second, reaching a maximum speed of 820 km/h with some 45-50 minutes endurance at 10,000 m. In reality, the *Volksflitzer* would have demonstrated significantly lower performance characteristics than the *Volksflugzeug*.

Junkers' submission rested on a design by Professor Heinrich Hertel, the firm's Head of

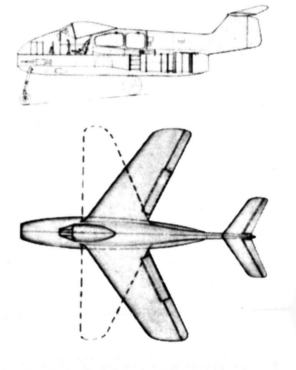

Volksflugzeug
BMW 003

Bewaffnung :	2 MK 108
Flügelfläche :	13,5 m^2
Fluggewicht :	2900 kg

Flugdauer (Vollast) :

| | 0 km Höhe | 0,5 Std. |
| | 10 km   " | 0,7 Std. |

Kraftstoffvorrat :   660 kg

LEFT The Focke-Wulf submission for the *Volksjäger* project took the form of an adaptable swept or unswept wing design with a long intake duct for a BMW 003 engine. However, the so-called *Volksflugzeug* was not considered as a serious proposal by the RLM

Aircraft Development. It is believed to have carried a ventral BMW 003, with high, unswept wings and a single tail fin. The design progressed to model stage, and is thought to have been assigned the design number EF 123 or EF 124. No armament information or technical specifications are known. Of the Junkers proposal to install a powerplant underneath the fuselage in order to attain a smaller surface of resistance, Heinkel and Frydag remarked to Allied interrogators in July 1945 that 'In our opinion this installation is dangerous in cases of forced landing and tends to catch fire. Besides, the powerplant beneath the fuselage would be destroyed in most cases of forced landing, whereas the powerplant over the fuselage (in the case of the He 162), as experience has shown, never led to accidents in forced landings.'

All tender proposals were delivered to the RLM in time, and on 14 September – the date of the deadline – representatives of all five competing companies gathered at the Ministry in Berlin for what was to be a two-day meeting with senior Luftwaffe technical officers and RLM officials. With blinding irony, chief among the RLM's assessors was none other than Dipl-Ing Carl Francke, Technical Director of EHAG at Vienna-Schwechat and Heinkel's representative at the meeting.

For its part, Heinkel had chosen to submit the P 1073-15 but with further modifications, the majority of which had been suggested by the company's engineering personnel at its Rostock-Marienehe plant. Siegfried Günter finalised this design as the P 1073-18, which had a high, unswept wing, twin fins and rudders and a BMW 003 mounted in a dorsal location on the fuselage. Armament comprised two MG 151/20 20 mm cannon fitted symmetrically in the forward fuselage, either side of the cockpit and below the pilot. The tricycle undercarriage was also retained, with the nosewheel retracting forward into the tip of the nose and ahead of the pilot. Together with 50 kg of armour plate, 145 kg of equipment, and allowance for a pilot at 90 kg, 'military' weight totalled 500 kg. With an airframe weight of 725 kg, the BMW 003 also at 725 kg and the fuel and fuel tank weighing 550 kg, the overall weight of the aircraft was foreseen at 2500 kg.

A model of the Junkers EF 123 or EF 124 'Developmental Aircraft' proposed by that firm as a contender for the *Volksjäger* project. Featuring a ventrally fitted BMW 003, with high, unswept wings and a single tail fin, the design failed to impress the RLM engineers

It was planned that such a machine could carry one SC 250 bomb as an offensive load, and there was an alternative armament configuration of two MK 108 30 mm cannon. Speed was calculated at 810 km/h at ground level, 860 km/h at 6000 m and 800 km/h at 11,000 m. Endurance was projected at 20 minutes at ground level and 33 minutes at 6000 m, while range would be 270 km at ground level and 440 km at 6000 m. Climbing speed was calculated at 22 metres per second at ground level, 13.5 metres per second at 6000 m and 4.5 metres per second at 11,000 m. The P 1073-18 would be able to take off from a 650 m runway.

The P 1073 came in for criticism from Dr-Ing Vogt of Blohm und Voss, who observed that despite Heinkel having a head start in the *Volksjäger* bid, the company had not adhered to the RLM's specification in terms of armament and endurance. Far from a 'simple-to-build' fighter, the P 1073 was actually very complex in its design, which would result in the need for dedicated cranes to be available at all operational airfields in order to remove and lift away the dorsally mounted engines. Furthermore, if removal of the P 1073's wings was required, the engine, its casing and fuel pipes had to be taken off first.

But when it came to discussing Blohm und Voss's P 211.02, according to Vogt, Francke 'gave only five minutes and sat timing it with his watch in his hand. It was obvious that he was not the least bit interested in this proposal. This, despite Oberstleutnant Knemeyer and his advisors, Oberstabsingenieur Malz of the RLM's single- and twin-engined fighter development section and Schwarz, the deputy leader of the Fighter Aircraft Development Group, collectively stating that the Blohm und Voss project had much to its credit, even though the weight given in the specification was slightly higher. However, this could have been solved through further discussion and further work.'

The proposals from Focke-Wulf were judged unrealistic, with a suspicion that the firm involved itself only for the purposes of gathering information on the efforts of its competitors, while the submissions from Arado and Junkers were completely rejected. Even the Heinkel P 1073-18 was regarded as unsuitable. The Blohm und Voss P 211-02 was judged to be

Generalingenieur Roluf Lucht (third from left), the head of the Development Commission for Aircraft and the most senior RLM officer to be closely involved with the *Volksjäger* project, joins Dipl-Ing Carl Francke (second from left) in September 1940 while Francke was serving with the Luftwaffe test centres to watch the first test flight of the Heinkel He 280 V1 jet aircraft. Francke would later serve as Technical Director of EHAG at Vienna-Schwechat. Also seen in this photograph, sixth from left, is the *Generalluftzeugmeister*, Ernst Udet

the best of the projects submitted, from both aerodynamic and engineering viewpoints. Francke protested that the other submissions had their weights and performances calculated by a different formula to that employed by his company, thus placing the Heinkel proposal in an unfavourable light.

The other participants duly recalculated the weights and performance of their proposals along the lines used by Heinkel. The revised specification from Blohm und Voss found favour with Oberst Diesing principally because the positioning of the engine did not obstruct the pilot's view, the design used less Duralumin in its construction – a material in short supply – and it could be assembled reasonably quickly. By contrast, the Heinkel design was again found to be lacking, both in terms of range and endurance. Its armament was also considered insufficient and there were concerns as to whether EHAG would be able to comply with the demands of production. Later in the meeting, however, the EHAG representatives managed to assure the panel that the company would be able to meet the delivery date requirement and would need fewer man-hours of construction. Capacity would be available following the cancellation of the He 177 bomber and the He 219 nightfighter. Furthermore, undercarriage legs from Bf 109s would be used, saving the need for new forgings, tools and wheels.

At this point, despite the inherent advantages in its construction, concerns began to arise regarding the Blohm und Voss P 211. It was thought that its long 2.5 m intake duct could be susceptible to power loss. Furthermore, its shape could induce drag, and because the air intake was only just over a metre off the ground, there was a risk of dirt and foreign bodies being ingested, resulting in engine damage – a very real prospect if the aircraft was to operate from rough, forward airfields.

So it was that after lengthy deliberation the Heinkel project won the day. At the conclusion of the meeting the projected programme was announced that aimed to have a mock-up inspection undertaken by 1 October 1944, with the first aircraft ready for takeoff by 10 December 1944 followed by the start of large-scale production in January 1945. By April 1945 production was planned to be at 1000 aircraft per month, increasing to 2000 per month thereafter.

Another meeting was held on 17 September to go over the matter again, but it proved inconclusive. Two days later, a third meeting was held under the chairmanship of Generalingenieur Roluf Lucht, the head of the Development Commission for Aircraft – a committee formed only four days earlier on the orders of Albert Speer – at which the Arado, Blohm und Voss and Heinkel projects were reviewed again, together with new submissions from Fieseler, Focke-Wulf, Junkers and Siebel. It was again agreed that the Blohm und Voss P 211-01 was superior in every respect to all other contenders, but the meeting ended in a heated argument between Heinkel's Karl Frydag, who disagreed with the decision, and Oberstabsingenieur Schwarz.

According to Vogt the Siebel proposal was hardly considered, and yet it was very evident that the Heinkel proposal had already been accepted beforehand without sufficient comparison with the Blohm und Voss proposal. Vogt noted;

'The manner in which these critical questions were dealt with during the committee meeting shook me to the core. It was impossible to speak of a review of the agenda topics, let alone a serious examination. Heinkel's Generaldirektor Frydag stated that the Blohm und Voss proposal contained a number of technical drawbacks, but no discussions regarding similar shortcomings to the Heinkel proposal were mentioned.'

Vogt concluded that as far as Blohm und Voss was concerned further time given to the *Volksjäger* project was pointless. In a last jab at the *Volksjäger* concept, members of Focke-Wulf's design team sent a memo to the RLM in which they urged caution;

'By the time it reaches the front in any meaningful numbers (third quarter of 1945), any *Volksjäger*-type aircraft is certain to be inferior to enemy jet fighters and its operational life span would be brief because: the BMW 003 is too weak a powerplant; the lack of wing sweep, dictated on production grounds, will limit dive speed and impair combat performance; there is no design capacity for improvements in armament, armour or other equipment.'

Meanwhile, EHAG had quietly finished work on a small-scale mock-up of the projected *Volksjäger* and invited the RLM to inspect it at their convenience.

On 21 September, the matter was the subject of a major conference of senior Luftwaffe commanders held at the OKL's forward headquarters in East Prussia. In attendance was Göring, Generaloberst Robert Ritter von Greim (the commander of *Luftflotte* 6) and Generalleutnant Karl Koller (the former Chief of the Luftwaffe Operations Staff), together with Galland, Diesing, Frydag, Lucht and Saur. Heinkel's design was favoured by Saur while Galland staunchly advocated the Me 262, as he recalled in his memoirs;

'From the beginning I had strongly opposed the *Volksjäger* project. In contrast to the creators of this idea, my objections were based on factual reasons such as insufficient performance, range, armament, poor visibility and dubious airworthiness. Furthermore, I was convinced that this aircraft could not be brought into worthwhile operation before the end of the war. The terrific expenditure of labour and material was bound to be at the expense of the Me 262. To my mind, all resources ought to be concentrated on this well-tested fighter in order to make the best of the possibilities remaining to us. If we scattered our strength once more in the last phase of the war, then all our efforts would be in vain.'

Two days later Hitler accepted Saur's advice and ordered the rapid mass production, without testing, of the Heinkel proposal at a provisional rate of 1000 machines per month by April 1945. Speer, also present at this meeting, noted that Hitler instructed the design to be carried forward with a 'vigorous drive' and with the manufacturer, the industrial and government authorities and the military all working with necessary coordination and cooperation.

That same day (23 September), Lucht and representatives of the Development Commission inspected the scale mock-up of the Heinkel P 1073 at Vienna-Heidfeld and were handed a freshly prepared ten-page report with accompanying drawings in which the design was described as a '*Strahljäger*' – a jet fighter. Armament was in the form of two MK 108s, each carrying 50 rounds, while the aircraft had an overall weight of 2571 kg and a maximum speed of 840 km/h at 6000 m, with a corresponding range of 430 km and an endurance of 33 minutes. At this point, the balance began to shift in Heinkel's favour.

Taking effect from 24 September, the Nazi production apparatus limbered up with fanatical energy. Hitler nominated Generalkommissar Phillipp Kessler, the director of a major electricity supplier and Chairman of the Armaments Advisory Board, as Kommissar of the '*Einstrahltriebkleinstjäger*' programme and of propulsion unit production. That May, Kessler had been awarded the Knight's Cross to the War Merit Cross with Swords for his vigorous contribution in sustaining ball-bearing production.

Shortly after, with the support of the Reich Youth Leader, Reichsleiter Artur Axmann, Saur proposed a scheme to provide the pilots required for the thousands of He 162 fighters that were expected to roll off the production lines in 1945. This was Generaloberst Keller's vision taking on a real dimension. He authorised an entire year's intake of the Hitler Youth to begin immediate glider training with the NSFK, after a short period of which they were to transfer directly to the He 162, but without any intermediate powered flying experience. Gunnery training was to be provided on the ground. According to Adolf Galland, 'Göring himself became a victim of the national frenzy with which the planning of the *Volksjäger* programme had infected almost everyone connected with air defence. "Hundreds! Thousands! Umpteen thousands!", exclaimed Göring, "until the enemy has been chased back beyond the borders of Germany".' In reality Göring had little influence in the matter since the decision to proceed with the *Volksjäger* had been taken by Hitler and Speer.

On 24 October, Lucht chaired a meeting to discuss training aircraft and also to examine how best to train for the He 162. In the case of the *Volksjäger*, discussion centred around the training of boys to become pilots, but somehow to do it without the need for fuel. It was thus recognised that there was a requirement for a towable, high-performance glider that would be comparable to a powered He 162, but which would be sparing of precious fuel. The meeting did not offer any immediate solutions, but it was proposed to investigate the matter further. The construction of such a machine was envisaged to be handled jointly between EHAG (allowing six weeks) and the NSFK (allowing a further six weeks), under the direction of the Development Commission.

It was planned to build ten such glider trainers by 29 December 1944. If these ten prototypes proved successful then the plan was to construct a further 200 examples. Each glider would weigh 400-500 kg and have a speed of four metres per second. The craft was to replicate, as far as possible, the takeoff and landing attributes of an He 162, using a 150 hp motorised winch which, with a 1000-m long cable, would release at 250 m. If the cable was extended to 1500 m, the winch could release at 400 m, which was considered sufficient for the pilot to acquire a feel for flight without having to leave the vicinity of an airfield. However, it was proposed that this could be increased to a release height of 1000 m using a 700 hp winch with a tow cable of 2500 m.

Like Galland, the bomber ace Oberstleutnant Werner Baumbach, who in late 1944 was posted to oversee the development and testing of guided weapons for the RLM before eventually being appointed as the *Kommodore* of KG 200, did not view these plans with enthusiasm. He recorded in his memoirs;

'I managed to convince nearly everyone of the absurdity of this idea. Even the He 162 called for thorough fighter training and could not "be flown by any Hitler Youth". But Saur continued to advocate his project with might and main, and no technical or other argument could convince him that the *Volksjäger* was no "people's fighter".'

On the last day of September 1944, Oberstleutnant Knemeyer formally announced the Heinkel proposal as the winner of the *Volksjäger* competition, ending all further discussion on the merits of its selection, despite continued protests from Dr-Ing Vogt of Blohm und Voss, who was advised of the decision by teleprinter message and whose P 211 was still facing problems with design. According to Vogt, Lucht apologised personally for not being aware of the fact that discussions had taken place directly between Frydag and Saur behind his back that had brought matters to a close. It appeared that Frydag's main grounds for objecting to the Blohm und Voss project was the positioning of its engine and its extended air intake, which would have had severe effects on the aircraft's performance.

During October, Professor Willy Messerschmitt expressed his feelings in a note prepared for Speer and Heinkel;

'The Me 262 must form the backbone of the Luftwaffe air defence in the deciding battles of the spring of 1945. The Me 262 is a reality, the *Volksjäger* only a hope. I cannot understand the need to develop a further aircraft when we already possess a superior machine. For about a year the Me 262 has been developed and parts are still required. Workmanship is lacking which endangers the performance of the machine, and yet while we are "screaming" for materials and parts, someone wants to develop a new aircraft.

'I regard the project for producing a cheap fighter with a BMW 003A propulsion unit for operational use in large numbers in the spring of 1945 as having [already] failed. The technical requirements postulated are erroneous, as the functions of the *Volksjäger* can be better carried out by already existing and proved aircraft. A development which does not conform in performance to existing technical possibilities is always behind the times. In my opinion there is not the slightest possibility that the *Volksjäger* programme can become sufficiently advanced by spring 1945 to warrant our counting on the aircraft becoming operational in large numbers. It is a delusion to think that the 162 can be developed and produced by "surplus manufacturing capacity" without disturbing production of current types and, in particular, the Me 262. Me 262 production is not yet well established. Jigs, skilled labour and control personnel are still lacking. The Me 262 is a really superior weapon, whilst the 162 is only a hope.'

Whilst the superiority, in most respects, of the Me 262 can be readily acknowledged, ironically, Messerschmitt's opinions serve only to lend some justification to the *Volksjäger* concept. By highlighting the delays affecting production of the Me 262, Messerschmitt was actually demonstrating his own 'delusion' of fast and reliable Me 262 output.

Because the German aviation industry tended to use a sizeable element of general-purpose, as opposed to specialised, machinery, a high proportion of skilled labour was required for the workforce. According to the *Aircraft*

Wind tunnel testing of the He 162 design began as early as October 1944, and by early 1945 had advanced on a significant scale at Göttingen, Braunschweig and the DVL at Berlin-Adlershof. The model seen here is being tested at the latter site

Industry Report of the US Strategic Bombing Survey, German airframe plants employed about 450,000 persons in October 1944. About 23 per cent, or 103,500, were women. The total number of Germans employed, both men and women, was only 52 per cent of the entire workforce. The remaining 48 per cent, or 216,000, comprised political prisoners, prisoners of war, Jews and foreign nationals of both sexes. Of the total workforce, some 36 per cent, or 162,000, were foreigners, many of whom were forced workers.

Furthermore, the Me 262 had been designed and developed to the production standards of 1940-43, which aimed at a 'zero defects' policy in manufacturing standards, and this only added to the difficulties resulting from the shortage of skilled labour. Series manufacture of the Me 262 had begun in March 1944, but owing to the fact that no other fighter type was taken out of production to ensure that the necessary labour and materials were released, only 122 machines had been completed by 10 August of that year.

In view of the Allies' air supremacy, the reduced training period for Luftwaffe fighter pilots and the poor reliability of the turbojet engines then available, a long service-life was not expected for jet aircraft. It was calculated that an Me 262 would be a total loss after five to ten combat missions. In addition, the Me 262 required two turbojet engines, and correspondingly more fuel, the supply of which was growing extremely scarce due to Germany's deteriorating military position. Thus, the concept of a single-engined turbojet fighter of about half the size and weight of the Me 262, but with a similar performance, became increasingly attractive on account of the potential savings in materials and production time. Because of design and load limitations, however, such a fighter, with only one powerplant, would not stand any chance of success unless compromises were made in its armament, armour, flight duration and equipment.

Nevertheless, by this time senior officers from the Staff of the *General der Jagdflieger* had begun to show interest in the new fighter concept. On 8 October, the Austrian Knight's Cross-holder Major Hartmann Grasser, a former *Jagddivision* commander and *Kommandeur* of III./JG 1 and II./JG 110, with 103 aerial victories to his credit, accompanied by Flg.Stabs.Ing Rauchensteiner, visited Heinkel to inspect the mock-up produced by his fellow countrymen. He was impressed.

By the end of the month Hitler had assigned the *Volksjäger* programme the highest priority, and, as a result, Günter and the Chief Designer at EHAG's Vienna and Rostock plants, Karl Schwärzler, worked tirelessly to oversee the completion of no fewer than 1000 detailed drawings, representing some 200,000 man-hours, by 5 November. This astonishing effort was brought about largely by EHAG dedicating its entire design staff of 370 men, including 50 designers and technicians, 143 draughtsmen and 50 stress men, to the He 162 at the expense of all other work. Many of the designers worked up to 90 hours per week and literally slept at their desks. Beyond the design work, some preliminary wind tunnel testing was also carried out at Göttingen. Thus it was that amidst an environment of hard work, innovation, competitive resentment and brooding hostility, the He 162 edged ever closer to reality

CHAPTER TWO

'WE HAD NOT RECKONED WITH SUCH LITTLE TIME'

Pools of dim light from overhead lamps cast shadows on the rock walls of the former chalk mine at Mödling, south of Vienna, which was used by EHAG as an underground factory for building He 162s. Codenamed '*Languste*', this view shows a worker pulling a section of fuselage over a mould, while carpenters use machine tools to process parts. In the background, another man operates a lathe. Workers would frequently spend hours in such conditions, with little exposure to daylight

At midday on 29 September 1944, amidst feelings of excitement, anticipation and, undoubtedly, some trepidation, Ernst Heinkel assembled his senior managers and engineers for a meeting at his villa in Vienna to discuss plans for production of the *Volksjäger* – or, as Heinkel saw it, for reasons of personal prestige, the 'He 500'. In attendance were Siegfried Günter, Karl Schwärzler, Otto Butter (Deputy Chief Designer), Karl Hayn (Senior Works Director), Ulrich Raue (Works Director at Schwechat) and Karl-Otto Burmeister (Senior Production Advisor). Carl Francke had returned from the meetings in Berlin and opened discussions with the proclamation, 'We have the contract for the *Kleinstjäger*. Proviso – first flight on 1 December 1944 and main series production by March 1945. We had not reckoned with such little time.'

This was the day before Knemeyer would make the formal announcement that Heinkel had won the contract to build the *Volksjäger*. The meeting took on an air of urgency, with Heinkel stating, 'We have to keep to the proposed schedule. All the people involved will still have duties to perform. I can get 150 construction workers from Messerschmitt.'

Günter responded with, 'From tomorrow I can deliver the first project documents and the rest can follow latest within two weeks.'

'By the end of December 1944 I must have all the essential construction information', Hayn explained. 'Then, by the end of January, I can deliver the necessary working proposals and by the end of February I will need all the tools and machinery so that from March I can deliver the series production.'

Heinkel noted, 'Before that I want to know when the prototype and drawings will be ready as we have only nine weeks before the first flight.'

'We can finalise the schedule when we have the project drawings', Schwärzler answered, angering Heinkel, who retorted, 'It's no good putting obstacles in the way – we have to move ahead as per schedule.'

'The earliest I can comment on this is tomorrow', Schwärzler replied.

Francke then asked Butter, 'When can you produce a list of all the material needed for the prototype, including drawings and parts?' Butter replied, 'We need five weeks for construction.' This prompted Raue to ask, 'If we need more than five weeks, can we run over? As from tomorrow we'll need all the support we can get.'

Butter replied, 'The construction schedule can be maintained, dare I say, if the following can be put in place – the necessary number of co-workers; a division of labour; construction alterations; and an understanding with department management over the need for overtime. I am concerned regarding the outsourced Messerschmitt workers. From my 450 men, I will search out the best 250 who will remain in the Fichtegasse office. All the others will be responsible for other work in the main office. As an incentive, we should get 10,000 cigarettes and 500 bottles of wine to distribute as a goodwill gesture.'

'I'd like the same as well', Raue requested.

Francke ended the meeting on a positive note. 'I believe that Butter and Raue can maintain the deadline as long as Dr Heinkel can agree.'

'I agree totally', affirmed Heinkel.

Despite Heinkel requesting the designation 'He 500', by 3 October the RLM had allocated the defunct type number '8-162' to the aircraft in a misguided attempt to confuse Allied intelligence as to the aircraft's true identity. Nevertheless, Heinkel immediately commenced work on the new machine.

On the 7th, another meeting was convened, this time at Heinkel's offices in Vienna, and which included design, technical and engineering representatives from none other than Messerschmitt, Junkers, Focke-Wulf and Dornier. The objective was to plan construction procedures, workforce organisation and delegation. All aspects of the proposed aircraft were discussed, including the fuselage, tail assembly and the connection of the tail assembly to the fuselage, wing-fuselage connections, functioning of the undercarriage, nosewheel hydraulics and door, armour plating, seat position, cockpit canopy, wings, controls and steering. The meeting concluded that more time might be needed to ensure adequate development of the various fixings and parts.

On 15 October, prototype drawings were issued to the workshops at Vienna-Heidfeld and jig and tool design moved ahead. But only four days later, the *Chef* TLR (*Technische Luftrüstung*, who occupied a senior position that saw him liaise between Speer's Ministry of Armament, the OKL and the Wehrmacht) asked for further changes in addition to those already requested, involving the BMW engine installation, wing configuration and the installation of the undercarriage and fuel tank. These centred on a redesign of the planned canopy jettisoning system, the installation of rocket-assisted takeoff (RATO) units and an enhanced oxygen system for high-altitude.

By this stage, officially, the He 162 featured a BMW 003 A-1 or E-1 engine and would be armed with either two Rheinmetall-Borsig MK 108 30 mm cannon (each with 50 rounds per gun) as the He 162A-1, or two Mauser MG 151/20 20 mm cannon (each with 120 rounds per gun) as the He 162A-2. It would be capable of a speed of 780 km/h, with an endurance of 57 minutes and a range of 660 km. A 960-litre fuel tank would be fitted and the aircraft was to be equipped with FuG 24Z and FuG 25a IFF radio equipment.

Production of the He 162 would be spread across EHAG's four plants at Rostock-Marienehe, Oranienburg, Barth and Vienna-Schwechat, the latter having a workforce of 8000 in September 1944. In Vienna, the company also requisitioned the facilities of neighbouring businesses – including the Schwechat Brewery, which allowed its cellars to be used for pattern making, mostly undertaken by 'political detainees'. Heinkel also engaged in collaborative work with the Junkers firm, which had surplus production capacity following the decrease in bomber output at this late stage of the war. Junkers would assume two-thirds of the production work for the He 162 at its plant at Bernburg, while decisions regarding tools and other preparatory measures would be a matter of cooperation between the two companies.

Like many Nazi projects, the He 162 was built on slave labour. Around 8000 forced labourers would be drafted in to work on the aircraft at Rostock, accounting for 55 per cent of the workforce there, while at Oranienburg the figure was even higher, with 5900 workers representing 65 per cent of total labour. The Vienna facilities would employ a further 2000 forced workers, accounting for 33 per cent of the available labour. Forty-five per cent of the workforce at Heinkel's partner, Junkers, was made up of forced labour, equating to 22,500 workers. At the infamous 'Mittelwerke' underground facility at Nordhausen, production of the He 162 progressed under the codename '*Schildkröte*' ('Tortoise'), using some 7000 malnourished slave labourers working in intolerable conditions alongside around 1000 Germans. The concentration camp at Ravensbrück would be a source of labour for the EHAG facility at Barth, while the Sachsenhausen and Mauthausen camps were able to supply Oranienburg and Schwechat/Heidfeld with additional 'workers'.

It was estimated that it would take 750 man-hours to complete one He 162 at the Mittelwerke, while 300 man-hours would be needed to build a BMW 003 turbo engine. Under such an infrastructure the output target was to be 1000 aircraft per month from each plant at Rostock-Marienehe, Vienna-Schwechat, Oranienburg, Bernburg and Nordhausen.

The He 162 project took on an even more sinister complexion when, as early as November 1944, it attracted the attention of senior figures within the SS. On the 9th, *SS-Obergruppenführer und General der Waffen-SS,*

Gottlob Berger, the *Chef des SS-Reichssicherheitshauptamt*, wrote to *Reichsführer-SS* Heinrich Himmler providing an outline of the production methods and the savings in raw materials that such methods were envisaged as offering.

In addition a group of 50 key employees would coordinate the activities of the assigned sub-contractors and parts-suppliers. This sprawling network would see fuselages made at an EHAG *Waldwerk* (forest factory) at Barth and at an underground facility at Mödling, in the Hinterbrühl. The latter, the site of a former chalk mine in Lower Austria 20 km south of Vienna, was codenamed '*Languste*' ('Crayfish'). Junkers would contribute from another underground facility, in this case a salt mine near Stassfurt.

Metal components would be sourced from Heinkel satellite facilities at Pütnitz (for Rostock) and Theresienfeld (for Vienna), while Junkers would source from Aschersleben, Stassfurt, Halberstadt, Leopoldshall and Schönbeck. Engines would come from BMW at Spandau and Zühlsdorf, while armaments would be supplied by the *Deutsche Waffen- und Munitionsfabrik* at Posnan on behalf of Rheinmetall-Borsig (for the MK 108) and Mauser at Oberndorf and Berlin (for the MG 151). Zeiss-Ikon would provide the Revi 16 gunsight from Berlin-Zehlendorf and Dresden, while Askania would supply the EZ 42 from Berlin-Friedenau. Paint would be sourced from both Austrian and German suppliers, while three main sub-contractors were selected for the manufacture of wooden components based at Neustadt an der Orla, Erfurt and Stuttgart-Esslingen. All three had previously undertaken work on wooden airframes such as the manufacture of wings for transport gliders and the Me 163 rocket-powered interceptor, as well as the all-wood Ta 154.

Construction work on the He 162 prototypes began on 25 October 1944, and by 1 November stability and functional experiments, the production of wind tunnel models as well as the preparation and evaluation of wind tunnel data and the writing of maintenance manuals for the He 162 were being carried out in Rostock. Just over a fortnight later, on the 17th, the EHAG Technical Department reported that the first prototype, the He 162 V1, was expected to roll out on schedule and that the wings and engine for the aircraft were to be moved to Vienna by road by the following Sunday. 'The rest of the parts are all on hand', Francke noted, and they 'could have been here a day or two earlier'. However, he did observe that there was not enough fuel to transport these parts. Furthermore, he recorded that, 'There are 50 too few German skilled workers for series construction in Vienna. Requirement not yet critical and the company will try to recruit as necessary.'

That same day, to the north at Rostock, Generalkommissar Kessler, running the '*Einstrahltriebkleinstjäger*' programme, chaired a conference intended to formally authorise the commencement of series production of the He 162 there and to coordinate local production facilities. Generally, things seemed to be moving ahead well, and yet there was some unease within EHAG following the completion of the first prototype. On 18 November Francke drafted a confidential memo to his management team, including Professor Heinkel, on a matter that was clearly bothering him;

'With the conclusion of the construction of the 162, remarks are being made that the Technical Department has nothing to do and could do without some of its personnel. There is so much development work in Vienna at this time that the personnel of the Technical Department are totally occupied, working a 72-hour week, plus overtime (72-hour weeks are not the practice at Messerschmitt, Focke-Wulf or Junkers). The number of staff of the Technical Department is laughably small in comparison to the staff of the other companies mentioned.'

Francke commented that his department was overseeing general project management, the planned installation of the BMW 003 and HeS 011 engines, the possibility of downward-swept wings, the construction of both powered and glider trainer versions and the building of other complex projects. He went on;

'I am not of the opinion that the 162 is the last development of this war, even for Heinkel. If the enemy appears with jets next spring that are somewhat faster than the 162 or 262, then we shall have to develop an aircraft quickly that is similar to the 162, but with swept-back wings and a more powerful engine. It was only possible to achieve the on-schedule development of the 162 because of the unconditional procurement of personnel from various jurisdictions. It would be foolish to now drop such an effective tool. In conclusion, it should be stated that the constant removal of poor personnel is the order of the day, but that the transfer or surrender of good personnel is not only inadvisable, but also dangerous. This is especially the case in regards to future transfers and call-ups for military service.'

The development of downward-swept wings to which Francke referred had been the design of Dr Alexander Lippisch, the acclaimed aerodynamicist who had been consulted by EHAG to improve lateral stability on the He 162. It was convenient that Lippisch, who had played an instrumental role in the development of the Me 163 rocket-powered interceptor whilst working for Messerschmitt in 1943, was at this time resident in Vienna, and therefore close at hand. Lippisch had proposed fitting small '*Ohren*' ('ears') to the wingtips of the He 162, and when incorporated into the design of the aircraft this distinctive feature became known as the 'Lippisch ears'.

Francke was still feeling under pressure on 21 November when he wrote to Generalstabs-Ingenieur Dipl-Ing Lucht at the RLM, who, since September 1944, had been chairman of the Emergency Aircraft Commission. Francke's communication is revealing;

'You intend to have a development meeting of the Commission on Friday of this week, which I am supposed to attend. Please inform my courier when and where this meeting is to take place so I can make the proper arrangements to attend. Because of the constant air raids on Vienna, communication

Clad in his former Luftwaffe leather greatcoat, Dipl-Ing Carl Francke (third from left), Technical Director of EHAG at Vienna-Schwechat, joins personnel from the Rostock plant on 14 January 1945 to watch the inaugural flight of the first He 162 to be completed at the site, Wk-Nr 120001. Also present, with his back to the camera in heavy ankle boots, is Richard Thiedemann, a senior manager of the Junkers plant at Bernburg

The pristine first prototype He 162 V1 Wk-Nr 200001 'VI+IA' was rolled out at Heidfeld on 1 December 1944. It was fitted with two MK 108 30 mm cannon and is seen here in its bare metal finish, which was later replaced by an overall coat of RLM 02

with the outside world is very limited. I need, at least, to be able to use the telephone so that the He 162 deadlines are not jeopardised.'

That same day Francke fired off a memo to a timber sub-contractor in Stuttgart who required an extension to a delivery deadline for wings. 'This is completely unacceptable. The wings for the prototypes, and series aircraft, are to be delivered on time'. The next day, Francke advised Heinkel and Frydag of his concerns about the timber firms appointed as sub-contractors;

'It is difficult to predict if the wood construction firms that we have hired (under the leadership of Dr-Ing May) will be able to fulfil their contracts in regards to wings, tail assemblies and flaps. However, we have already observed how inflexible the firms that we have hired are in regards to development and prototype construction. Furthermore, they lack skilled workers.'

Dr-Ing May, in charge of coordinating Heinkel's timber suppliers and sub-contractors from Berlin, again incurred Francke's wrath later that day following receipt of a telegram regarding a particular supplier;

'It seems there has been non-delivery of metal fittings and delay on the 162 wing. The Kalkert concern also lacks the parts needed. Dr-Ing May is not screaming for the parts because he knows he can use the excuse of non-delivery to delay his own deadline. The distribution of completed sub-assemblies on our part is not working. I suggest that a man be found here in Vienna who will be able to deal with the problem. We cannot afford to allow the timber workshops, whose deliveries are way off, to blame us for the delays.'

Despite these setbacks, on the 24th, Francke noted that, mercifully, the He 162 V1 prototype was 'nearing completion'. Its wings had been fitted, although the metal parts had not been finished correctly by EHAG. Furthermore, its engine had been damaged in transit. Any notion of a restful end to the day was cast aside when Francke was forced to despatch

Flugkapitän Dipl-Ing Gotthold Peter was chief test pilot at EHAG at the time of the He 162's development. Born in Dresden in 1912, he joined Heinkel in August 1940 after having worked for Arado. Involved in flight-testing the He 177 bomber and He 219 nightfighter prototypes, Peter was the first man to fly the He 162 – but with fatal consequences

A still from a cine film showing what is believed to be the He 162 V1 at Heidfeld as it taxies past a gathering of EHAG workers just before takeoff on its maiden flight on 6 December 1944. Generally, it was a successful flight

a telegram in which he used no fewer than ten exclamation marks to complain about yet another apparent collapse in basic communication within his own workforce over parts supply. 'Insane! Can you believe it?' he wrote.

Francke's tolerance was subjected to further test on the 27th when, at last, the first tail unit arrived for fitting to the prototype;

'The first tail unit has arrived after a difficult journey and was attached, thank God! It has been installed into the V1, but it doesn't fit! A substitute is being arranged.'

In what represented a Herculean effort, however, on 1 December 1944 the first prototype of the He 162, V1 (later M1) Wk-Nr 200001, was completed, fitted with MK 108 cannon and made ready for takeoff at Heidfeld less than 70 days after the authorisation of the *Volksjäger* programme. Schwärzler, however, expressed concerns about the weakness of the undercarriage and, as a result, only taxiing trials were undertaken the next day. Meanwhile, also on the afternoon of the 1st, Hauptdienstleiter Dipl-Ing Karl-Otto Saur, the originator of the *Volksjäger* concept, journeyed to Lärz airfield and inspected a wooden mock-up of the He 162.

The He 162 V1 first took to the air on 6 December, five days ahead of schedule, with Heinkel's chief test pilot, Flugkapitän Dipl-Ing Gotthold Peter, at the controls. The aircraft, fitted with two MK 108 cannon, performed well aside from the fact that one of the mainwheel doors broke away as a result of defective bonding. The BMW engine also ran well and Francke recorded, no doubt with some relief as well as satisfaction, 'No basic problems'.

At 'Languste' things were moving ahead apace, with the V2, V3 and V4 all undergoing final assembly, and the V2 being transported to Heidfeld on the 7th in readiness for testing. The only real area of concern on all the prototypes centred around the wings, which were found to be weak as a result of some 'leaking'. Initially, a soft shellac had been used as a sealant, but when this was found to 'leak' it was replaced by a putty. Heinkel recognised, however, that it would probably be impossible to rectify the problem completely.

Nevertheless, Francke remained worried over the question of glue, as well as over the weight of the V1, which was 17 kg heavier than had been projected by the engineers. 'This overweight needs to be stripped out', he commented in his report of the 7th. His fears were to be proved justified on the 10th when catastrophe struck the He 162 programme.

That day a group of senior Luftwaffe officers and Armaments Ministry officials arrived at Schwechat to observe Gotthold Peter make another test flight in the V1. Whilst aloft, Peter attempted an unscheduled, low-level, high-speed run over the airfield. At around 735 km/h the leading edge, halfway along the starboard wing, ripped away, causing the aircraft to go into a roll, which broke away the aileron and wing tip. At such a low altitude Peter was unable to escape the aircraft, which crashed out of control beyond the airfield boundary near Fischamend. He was killed instantly.

The Heinkel team was fortunate in that the whole episode had been caught on cine-film by an officer on the staff of General Galland who had been sent to Schwechat to observe the flight of the *Volksjäger* and then report back to the *General der Jagdflieger*. Study of the film revealed that there had been instability around the aircraft's lateral axis, which, combined with a lack of glue bonding, resulted in the tearing away of the wing component. Thus, the wings were to be strengthened immediately and a speed restriction of 500 km/h imposed on all subsequent test flying.

The loss of Peter and the V1 was a blow to the EHAG development team, but they worked hard to analyse the faults and to introduce improvements to the build of the aircraft. These included an increase in the span of the horizontal stabiliser, displacement of the centre of gravity by shortening the main fuel tank, the strengthening of wing ribs and their attachment to the main beam and the strengthening of wing coverings. The knock-on effect of this was to prevent any further aircraft beyond the few prototypes already under construction being delivered in January and February. Furthermore, the wing leakage problems had still not been solved by 15 December. Tests with water had already been conducted by the sub-contractors manufacturing the wings, who complained that the recommended sealing compound could no longer be obtained.

Nevertheless, on the 20th, He 162 M3 Wk-Nr 200003 'V1+IC' was reported as flight-ready and was moved from Languste to Heidfeld, while two days later Francke himself was airborne for the first flight of He 162 V2/M2 Wk-Nr 200002 'VI+IB', which had been fitted with a MK 108

Flugkapitän Gotthold Peter flies He 162 V1 'VI+IA' over the heads of senior Luftwaffe officers and Armaments Ministry officials at Schwechat on 10 December 1944. Peter attempted an unscheduled low-level, high-speed pass over the airfield

Caught on film – the moment He 162 V1 Wk-Nr 200001 was rolled by Flugkapitän Gotthold Peter, causing the centre section of the leading edge of the starboard wing to tear away. The aileron and wingtip followed shortly thereafter. Investigation revealed that the aircraft had suffered from instability around its lateral axis, which, combined with a lack of glue bonding, resulted in Gotthold Peter's death

cannon. Aside from his role as EHAG's Technical Director at Schwechat, Francke, as one of the most experienced test pilots in Germany, was more than qualified to fly the aircraft and he felt a personal obligation to do so following the crash of the V1. During their discussions with former EHAG personnel shortly after the war, Allied interrogators were told that such a flight was indicative of 'the character of the man heading the team responsible for the development of the He 162'.

Francke's flight proved largely trouble-free, and he was followed the same afternoon by Fliegerstabsing Paul Bader of the RLM's test centre at Rechlin in a sortie that lasted six minutes. Apparently Francke and Bader had tossed a coin to decide who would first be in the air and Francke had won. For his part, Bader had considerable experience in test-flying jet aircraft, having flown the He 280 prototypes and the Me 262 V1, and on 22 December he was appointed *Typenbegleiter* ('Project Leader' or 'Development Coordinator') for the He 162 programme.

In the wake of Gotthold Peter's fatal flight, however, Bader was ordered to keep speed to under 500 km/h. He found that loaded with 450 litres of fuel and a full compliment of ammunition, the aircraft handled like a much larger jet, but there was some unpleasant 'snaking' experienced during takeoff and landing. He also noted that forward visibility on the ground from the cockpit was so poor that the only clear way to see ahead was to 'snake' the aircraft manually. Furthermore, even with the canopy closed, he was aware of exhaust fumes entering the cockpit. The flight itself, however, was problem free.

At this point it was planned that the He 162 V2 would be used to trial takeoffs and landings and for the testing of rudder stability, while the V3 would be fitted with a modified nosewheel leg to prevent ground looping. It was also envisaged that the V4 would fly at the end of the year, while the V6 was to be fitted with a strengthened wing, and to fly ten days after the new wing had been delivered. Wind tunnel tests showed that the critical Mach number for the He 162 was 0.72 and that a cap on top speed of 870 km/h should be put in place.

He 162 M4 Wk-Nr 200004 'VI+ID', fitted with MK 108s, was reported flight-ready at Languste on the 29th, but M5 Wk-Nr 200005 'VI+IE'

Fliegerstabsingineur Paul Bader from the RLM test centre at Rechlin flew He 162 M3 Wk-Nr 200003 'VI+IC' at Heidfeld on 20 December 1944. Despite a trouble-free flight, he was of the opinion that forward visibility for the pilot was very poor. Bader was appointed development coordinator for the He 162 programme shortly afterwards

A view of an He 162 cockpit simulator mock-up built by the Luftwaffe's test centre at Rechlin in November 1944. It appears that the engine instrument gauges – temperature, fuel pressure, fuel level and rpm – are connected, indicative that the simulator was being used for engine-testing, while the other instruments have been taped over

had beaten it by five days, although this machine would never fly and no weapons were fitted to it.

As 1945 dawned, the M4 was rolled out on 4 January, ready to be flown by Dipl-Ing Schuck. He was authorised to fly the aeroplane at speeds up to 500 km/h, but this would not take place until the 16th when the jet would have ballast loaded in its nose and would partake in stability tests and roll trials, with strengthened wings and fuselage. Fitted with the strengthened wings, the aircraft would actually attain 700 km/h. The same day of the M4's flight, the M3 was flown by former bomber pilot Leutnant Huldreich Kemnitz, who undertook takeoff, landing and vibration trials. On the 10th, He 162 M18 Wk-Nr 220001 'VI+IK' was declared flight-ready at Languste and moved to Heidfeld. This aircraft was actually the A-01, intended as a pre-production machine for the planned A-2 series. It was equipped with two MG 151/20 20 mm cannon and carried added ballast in its nose section with the aim of shifting its centre of gravity. The aircraft would be used to test takeoff and landing characteristics, in-flight endurance and radio and camera installations.

In late November 1944 engine technicians at the Luftwaffe's test centre at Rechlin constructed a simulator intended to replicate the functioning of the He 162's controls and the BMW 003 engine in combat. This photograph of the rig also provides a good view of the BMW engine

Partially completed He 162 fuselages rest in mobile cradles in the Heinkel cave factory at Mödling awaiting fitment of engines. In the fuselage in the foreground, the breech block for the right-side MK 108 cannon can just be seen where the access panel has been removed

A technician works on the wiring of an He 162 fuselage at the Languste factory. The low headroom and closeness of the rock walls must have made for a claustrophobic and oppressive atmosphere

January would see increased testing activity. On the 16th, He 162 M3 'VI+IC', which had been intended to assess general flight characteristics, flew with 'Lippisch ears' fitted to its reinforced wings as well as an enlarged tail assembly. This aircraft would undertake a remarkable 13 test flights in one week and would ultimately reach a top speed of 880 km/h. Also on this day, He 162 M19 Wk-Nr 220002 'VI+IL' was declared flight-ready.

Forty-eight hours earlier, on 14 January, the EHAG plant at Rostock had reported its first He 162 ready in the form of Wk-Nr 120001, which made its inaugural flight lasting 14 minutes with unstrengthened wings. A number of further flights took place once a radio unit had been installed and no subsequent problems were encountered. Two days later, Wk-Nr 120002 left final assembly without strengthened wings and awaiting a tail assembly. It was planned to flight-test the aircraft on 22 January. At Vienna on the 17th, He 162 M6 Wk-Nr 200006 'VI+IF', which was to be the pre-series machine for the A-1 type, was reported ready to assess stability, rudder functioning and weapons firing.

On the 18th, the M3 made its third flight, while He 162 M20 Wk-Nr 220003 'VI+IM' became flight-ready and was designated as an A-03. Its principal feature was a simplified undercarriage, and it was used to assess in-flight performance, centre of gravity, flaps and rudders, but it suffered damage four days later when its port wing collapsed on landing. On the 20th the M4 made its fourth test flight, although it too was damaged when the aircraft ploughed into deep snow. It was estimated that the necessary repairs would take two days to complete. Meanwhile, on 21 January, He 162 M21 Wk-Nr 220004 'VI+IN' was delivered from Languste to Heidfeld. Two days later, He 162 M6 Wk-Nr 200006 'VI+IF' was airborne for the first time, having been completed on 18 January. The aircraft was assigned to conduct weapons trials with two MK 108 cannon in readiness for the planned He 162A-1.

With its canopy raised, the first He 162A-1 (Wk-Nr 120001) to be completed at EHAG Rostock is prepared for flight on 14 January 1945. Note the parachutes placed on the nose of the aircraft

Disappointment had surrounded the arrival at Heidfeld of He 162 M18 (A-01) Wk-Nr 220001 'VI+IK' from Languste when it was discovered that there were more than 50 deviations from the type drawings, all of which had to be rectified before the machine was able to make its maiden flight. However, with these faults eventually fixed, the aircraft took to the skies on 24 January and was assigned to conduct roll tests, takeoff and landing tests and – as an He 162A-2, fitted with MG 151/20s – trials with a BMW 003 E-1 engine. That same day, He 162 M7 Wk-Nr 200007 'VI+IG' was moved from Languste to Heidfeld, this aircraft being fitted with two MG 151s, and He 162 M22 Wk-Nr 220005 'VI+IO' was delivered as an A-2.

By 27 January He 162A-01 Wk-Nr 220001 'VI+IK' (formerly the M18) had been declared flight-ready and made ten starts to assess general flight performance. Some play in the nosewheel strut was reported and the brakes proved temperamental. That same day, the M6 took off on a flight test that had to be abandoned due to engine failure when, at between 5000 and 7000 rpm, the pilot reported a 'grinding noise'. EHAG was forced to concede that the engine would need to be examined and probably changed.

An unidentified test pilot climbs into the cockpit of He 162A-1 Wk-Nr 120001 at Rostock-Marienehe. The aircraft performed a series of largely trouble-free test flights in January 1945

He 162 M6 Wk-Nr 200006 'VI+IF' streaks down the runway at Vienna-Schwechat at the start of a test flight on a wintry day in early 1945. In late January EHAG reported that this aircraft's engine would need to be examined and probably changed after grinding noises had been heard during a test flight

To the north at Rostock, He 162 Wk-Nr 120003 was still in final assembly, but unlike its local predecessors, this aircraft had strengthened wings. It was scheduled to be handed over for flight-testing on 23 January. The next day He 162 M23 Wk-Nr 220006 'VI+IP' moved from Languste to Heidfeld to commence general flight-testing.

Despite the increasingly frenetic pace of testing, the *Volksjäger* programme was dogged throughout the second half of January by delays in the delivery of strengthened wing sets, of which only 15 had been produced by the 21st. This in turn had an adverse effect on prototype production. Tail assembly also ran late, affecting output at Heidfeld, and the catastrophic transportation bottlenecks within the Reich resulted in ever-increasing delays to deliveries of components. Despite this, there is evidence that demands were being piled on the project team. On the 26th, for example, Francke enquired of his designers whether three or four He 162s could be fitted out as '*Behelfs-Aufklärer*' – improvised or emergency reconnaissance variants – and whether such machines could be ready by February. He must have known that that would be unlikely.

Things were little better at Rostock, where an inspection of the plant revealed the planned delivery of 30 aircraft had not been possible due to a lack of engines and wings. Just two He 162s had actually made it into the air and only 12 had finished engine tests. Yet a total of 139 fuselages were either completed or nearing completion. The plant had ground to a virtual standstill because the required tail units, when finally delivered, were found to be faulty. Furthermore, in Vienna, 12 Heinkels had been ready for some time but again they could not be delivered due to the supply of faulty parts. The reality was that only 14 machines had been completed across the board by 31 January.

By early February the parts situation at Rostock was also dire. Only 36 sets of wings were available against a planned 47 sets, 42 engines against a planned 47, 67 undercarriage mechanisms against a planned 81 and 24 sets of weapons-bay access panels against a planned 67 (*text continues on page 46*).

34

COLOUR PLATES

1
He 162 V1 Wk-Nr 200001 'VI+IA', Vienna-Schwechat, December 1944

2
He 162A-1 Wk-Nr 310001, Bernburg, February 1945

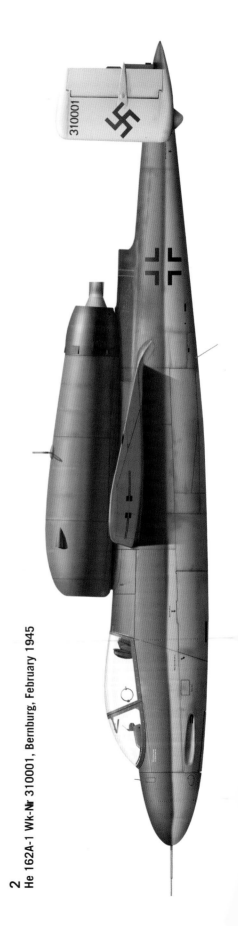

2
He 162A-1 Wk-Nr 310001, Bernburg, February 1945

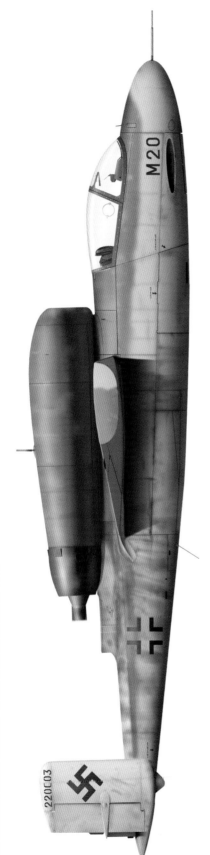

3
He 162 M20 *W*k-Nr 220003 'VI+IM', Lechfeld, March 1945

4
He 162S of the *Reichssegelflugschule*, Trebbin, March 1945

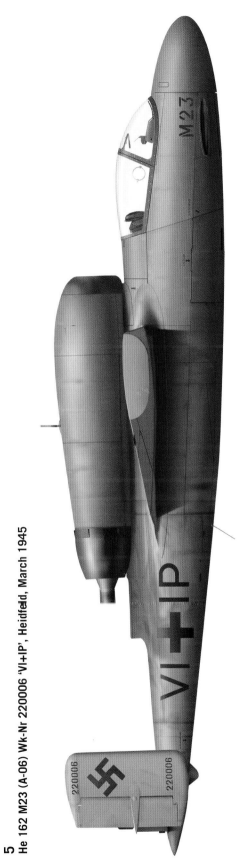

5
He 162 M23 (A-06) Wk-Nr 220006 'VI+IP', Heidfeld, March 1945

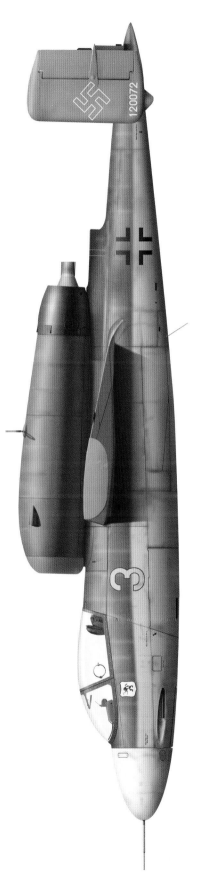

6
He 162A-2 Wk-Nr 120072 'Yellow 3' of 3./JG 1, Ludwigslust, April 1945

7
He 162A-1 Wk-Nr 12001(?) 'White 21' of 1./JG 1, Ludwigslust, April 1945

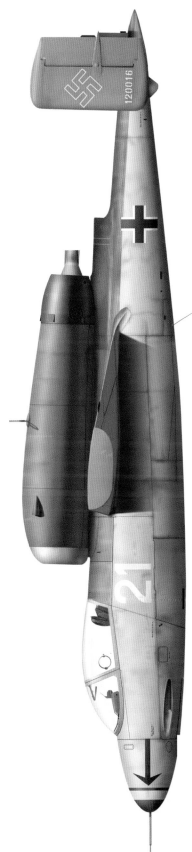

7
He 162A-1 Wk-Nr 120016(?) 'White 21' of 1./JG 1, Ludwigslust, April 1945

8
He 162A-2 Wk-Nr 120077 'Red 1' of 2./JG 1, Leck, April 1945

9
He 162A-2 possibly Wk-Nr 120013 'White 1' of 1./JG 1, Leck, May 1945

9
He 162A-2 possibly Wk-Nr 120013 'White 1' of 1./JG 1, Leck, May 1945

10
He 162A-1 possibly Wk-Nr 310078 'White 5' of 1./JG 1, probably Leck, May 1945

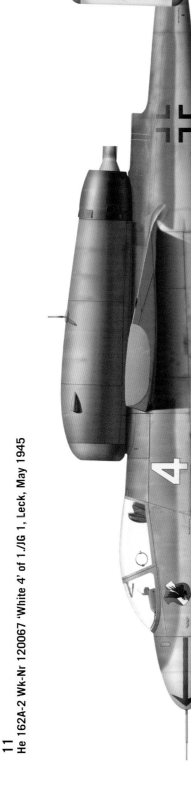

11
He 162A-2 Wk-Nr 120067 'White 4' of 1./JG 1, Leck, May 1945

12
He 162A-2 Wk-Nr 120074 'Yellow 11' of I./JG 1, Leck, May 1945

13
He 162A-2 Wk-Nr 120230 'White 23' of *Stab* JG 1, Leck, May 1945

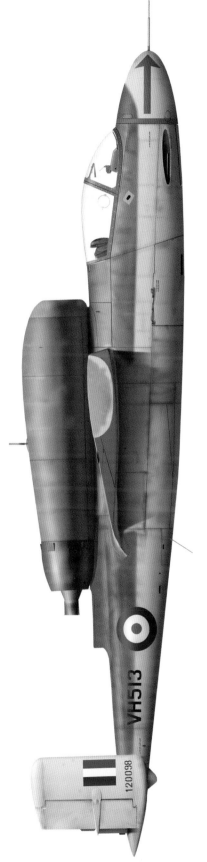

14
He 162A-2 Wk-Nr 120098, recoded VH513/AM 67, RAE Farnborough, September 1945 (possibly formerly 'White 2' of JG 1 at Leck)

14
He 162A-2 Wk-Nr 120098, recoded VH513/AM 67, RAE Farnborough, September 1945 (possibly formerly 'White 2' of JG 1 at Leck)

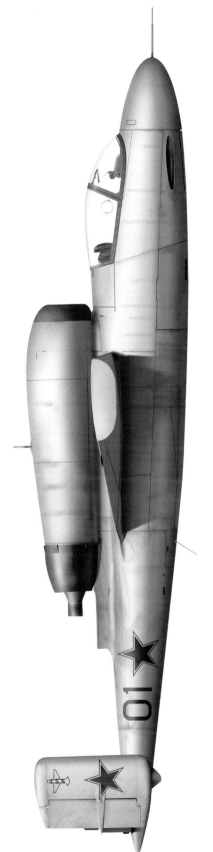

15
He 162A-2 'Red 01', LII, Moscow, spring 1946

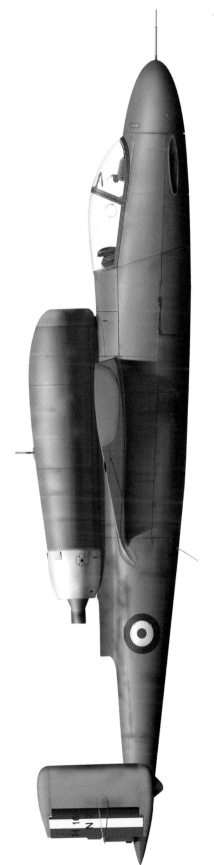

16
He 162A-2 No 2, SNCAC, Orléans-Bricy, 1947 (formerly 'White 21' of 1./JG 1)

A fellow pilot prepares to close the canopy of an He 162 with Oberleutnant Georg Wedemeyer at the controls at Schwechat. Note the smiling face painted onto the engine intake cover

The canopy is closed above Georg Wedemeyer's head, and in this still the engine intake cover has been removed ahead of imminent flight

The shortages also extended to nosewheels, main gear and nosewheel doors, rudders and other key parts such as nose cones and weapons access panels, all due from timber sub-contractors. Finally, of the wings that had been delivered in consignments between 17 and 20 January, five sets had major faults such as leaking fuel tanks, poor gluing and wrongly constructed components.

As if there was not enough to contend with, orders were received that from 29 January, for a period of eight days, the Rostock plant would have to close due to lack of electricity supply. The plant had been enduring problematic electricity supply for some time, resulting in the local management being compelled to 'demand' 20 hours of power per day in order to function, with the four-hour shutdown period being between 1700 hrs and 2100 hrs. High-speed flight-testing at Rostock had also been restricted due to bad weather and a lack of fuel.

By early February no completed aircraft had been delivered from the plant, although 12 machines had been signed off as far as engine serviceability was concerned. Furthermore, 20 engines, plus nosewheels, canopies and 27 FuG 24 radio sets, were outstanding. 'The completion of further aircraft', warned a senior engineer at Marienehe on 5 February, 'hangs in the balance pending the arrival of these missing parts.'

Despite all these odds, before January was out the A-01 made three good flights. Behind these came He 162 M19 A-02 Wk-Nr 220002 'VI+IL', with which it was intended to test stability of ailerons at high altitude as well as stability across the lateral axis. However, EHAG observed that the rudder trimming was not functioning and that the aircraft was subject to excess stress. Furthermore, the fuel lever brake did not pull and it was recommended that before the aircraft fly again, ballast should be placed in the nose. In later trials, however, this aircraft would attain a top speed of only 480 km/h due to poor stability around its lateral axis.

On the 30th, He 162 M26 Wk-Nr 220009 'VI+IS' (an A-2 with MG 151/20 cannon), built with an extended fuselage, was announced flight-ready. Both it and the M18 made a total of nine starts, these aircraft being assigned the job of testing a proposed ejector seat for the He 162. The M4 had been fitted with new wings with downward-pointing tips and would be ready for flight the next day. The M6 had been fitted with an extra 5 kg of weight to assist with rudder control, and this was found to be reasonably satisfactory. The M7 was undergoing compass alignment and stability tests while the M19 would be ready for flight on the 31st after having ballast loaded into its nose. The M20 underwent engine tests and steering modifications and was fitted with 45-degree downward-pointing wingtips so as to be ready for flight on 1 February.

By 4 February there had been 29 takeoffs in He 162s from Vienna, accounting for 7 hours 33 minutes of flying time. Seventeen starts had taken place on the 4th alone using the M3, M4, M6 and M18, with Francke, Bader, Hauptmann Horst Geyer from the staff of the *Kommandeur der Erprobungsstellen* and formerly commander of *Erprobungskommando* 25 (the weapons testing and evaluation unit), Oberleutnant Georg Wedemeyer and Leutnant Kemnitz of the RLM, Flugkapitän Bartels from DLH and test pilots Dipl-Ing Schuck, Ing Meschkat and Flugbaumeister Full and Gleuwitz all flying. Following its flight on the 4th the M3 required the installation of radio equipment, ballast to compensate for a full tank of fuel, weights to ease stick control, improvements to the rudder trim and 10 mm trimmed off the rear edge of the horizontal stabiliser. The M4 would continue to conduct takeoff, landing and stability tests, while the M18 was fitted with a camera to assess undercarriage functioning.

To date, the entire test programme, across all sites, had accumulated a total of 86 takeoffs, with a flying time of 16 hours and 33 minutes – an indication that testing of the He 162 was still in its infancy. The M4 and M19 were undergoing minor improvements to their stability, and following these improvements Hauptmann Geyer had flown the former machine with no problems. Also on the plus side, Kessler had arranged for 100 student workers from Pomerania to be available at Rostock in February, and they would each be assigned to an individual instructor working in electrics, mechanics, fitting and aircraft maintenance.

On 4 February another fatality struck the programme when the experienced test pilot Oberleutnant Wedemeyer crashed in the M6 during its 11th test flight at Schwechat. Wedemeyer, who had been born on 10 March 1910 in Westphalia, had been flying with the Luftwaffe

Oberleutnant Georg Wedemeyer was a veteran bomber pilot who saw action over Poland, Norway, England, Crete and Russia before joining EHAG, where he became a test pilot. He was killed flying the He 162 M6 on 4 February 1945

He 162 M20 Wk-Nr 220003 'VI+IM' photographed in a semi-derelict state at Munich-Riem shortly after the end of the war. The M20 featured a simplified undercarriage and was used to assess in-flight performance, centre of gravity and flaps and rudder functioning, but suffered a port wing collapse during testing in late January 1945. It was probably one of the ten machines flown out of Vienna to Lechfeld in early April in the face of the Soviet advance on the city

since 1934. That year he was posted to the *Fliegerschule* at Tutow as an instructor, and from the end of 1934 he served as a bomber pilot with KG 4. Wedemeyer saw combat over Poland, Norway, England, Crete and Russia, following which, in late 1941, he joined Heinkel. He had subsequently test flown the He 177, He 219 and He 280. Awarded the Iron Cross First Class, Wedemeyer was a married man with three children.

His aircraft had been seen to go into a curved dive, but the actual reason for the crash was not clear, although a seized rudder was suspected. Later, it was discovered that some of the plywood covering on the ribs of the M6's tail unit had not been glued adequately. An angry Ernst Heinkel declared that such crashes would not be tolerated and demanded that the strongest of complaints be made to the appropriate party regarding the poor workmanship involved. Blame was attributed to a sub-contractor at Weitramsdorf. Heinkel further ordered that landing flaps and other wooden parts produced by all sub-contractors be subjected to the closest scrutiny before acceptance, and that on any future occasion poor quality from outside suppliers would not be an acceptable excuse. To this end, he proposed that a department from the construction office for the now-abandoned He 219 be appointed as a controlling and instructing body to supervise all procedures in Vienna.

On 4 February Wk-Nr 009 was flown by both Flugkapitäne Heinrich and Sulzbacher, on each occasion with faultless performance. However, the two available airworthy aircraft at Rostock were subsequently dismantled and sent by rail to the Lufthansa facility at Oranienburg, with some parts transferred to Ludwigslust, where they were used to convert other aircraft to the latest specification.

Four days later there was another crash when Flugbaumeister Full had to force-land off the airfield at Schwechat following an engine failure while flying the M4 at 8000 m at a speed of 800 km/h conducting stability and dive tests. The aircraft, which was armed with MG 151s and fitted with strengthened wings and the new, down-turned 'Lippisch ear' wingtips, suffered 40 per cent damage. In the light of Full's crash, and the dangerous instability affecting the He 162's lateral axis, Francke ordered that further speed limitations be imposed on test flights.

Flugkapitän Ing. Hermann Steckhan prepares to seat himself in the cockpit of He 162 Wk-Nr 310001 at Junkers' Bernburg plant in February 1945

Pedal power! In an image of supreme irony, a bicycle is used to tow He 162 Wk-Nr 310001 out towards the runway at Bernburg. Flugkapitän Ing Steckhan recalled one acceptance flight in this aircraft on 28 March 1945 in which he suffered severe engine vibrations, but nevertheless continued safely with the flight

By mid-February Heidfeld was suffering similar power problems to Rostock, but if anything on a greater scale. During the period 17 January to 10 February the facility was without power for 104 hours. Furthermore, EHAG was running short of fuel with which to function, urgently requesting 1500 litres of petrol and 4000 litres of diesel, as well as two lorry trailers in which to store gas for emergency power generators. Even performing the most basic operations was becoming a challenge, with the condition of the grass taxiway from the hangars to the runway takeoff point at Heidfeld having deteriorated into a very muddy and rutted surface. Indeed, it was so bad that during a taxi run the M20 sank into mud between a hangar and the runway, risking major damage.

Transport was also a major problem. Due to Allied bombing raids, train schedules were badly disrupted and EHAG was compelled to use a small bus to transport key personnel in an emergency. Stocks of food and drink also had to be stockpiled as safely as possible in case of need.

On 13 February, in the sixth such attack of 1945, bombers from the USAAF's Fifteenth Air Force targeted depots and railway repair sheds in Vienna. It was to be the first of three consecutive daylight raids against railway yards and oil refineries in and around the city. He 162 M31

Wk-Nr 220014 'VI+IX' – a reserve aircraft that had carried out trials with a gyroscopic gunsight – was destroyed in the attack, having been completed only five days earlier.

With the very likely prospect of more frequent Allied raids, a heavily disrupted transport system and supply difficulties, production figures now had to be reassessed on the basis of reality, not wishful thinking. Furthermore, there was a reliance upon prisoner labourers who lacked motivation and often skill, and who suffered from malnourishment while working in long shifts in cramped, poorly organised underground facilities. The target figures were revised to an output of ten machines per month by 2 March from Heidfeld, ten per month by 5 March from Rostock and ten per month from Junkers at Bernburg by 10 March, where He 162s were now being built. Flugkapitän Ing Hermann Steckhan, a Junkers factory pilot, flew Bernburg's first He 162, Wk-Nr 310001, for 20 minutes during the late afternoon of 15 February, and six days later he flew Wk-Nr 310002 for ten minutes. All seems to have gone well.

Steckhan, who would fly the He 162 on more that 20 occasions, recounted one incident at Bernburg in which, having started one aircraft, he decided the machine did not 'feel right'. During taxiing, the aircraft continued to veer off to one side. He aborted the flight and taxied back to the hangar, whereupon he informed the engineers of the problem. The engineers shrugged their shoulders. Steckhan promptly grabbed a large saw and cut off the wingtip, peering into the exposed framework of the wing to observe that the timbers used were far larger than had been specified.

At Vienna, somehow the management kept things going. On 17 February both He 162 M25 (A-08) Wk-Nr 220008 'VI+IR' and M26 (A-09) Wk-Nr 220009 'VI+IS' took to the air for the first time, the former with Feldwebel Gleuwitz at the controls. The next day M28 (A-011) Wk-Nr 220011 and M29 (A-012) Wk-Nr 220012 made their maiden flights, both with extended and strengthened airframes and fitted with MK 108 cannon, from Heidfeld.

The test programme pushed on throughout February and into March 1945. There was a setback on 25 February when M3 Wk-Nr 200003, which had achieved a speed of 880 km/h during flight-testing, crashed east of Schwechat airfield while being flown by Flugbaumeister Full. Once again blame focused on instability around the aircraft's lateral axis. A witness on the ground reported that Full had attempted to bail out at 200 metres, but that his parachute was on fire.

Despite all the adversity, by late February 1945 the once mighty Third Reich, which had crumbled almost to its core, was still showing defiance. Neither the Rhine in the west nor the Oder in the east had been crossed, although the Russians had managed to seize bridges spanning the latter river. Nevertheless, when Adolf Hitler addressed his Gauleiters in Berlin on the 24th, he told them, 'You may see my hand tremble sometimes today and perhaps even my head now and then, but my heart – never!'

However, these sentiments did not reflect reality, and they did not stop EHAG from making plans to move its technical department from Vienna to Rostock, where conditions were judged to be somewhat safer. This, just at the time when the Luftwaffe was preparing to take on and deploy the He 162.

CHAPTER THREE

TRAINING AND TRIALS

A two-seat glider trainer version of the He 162, the 'S', was planned to train prospective pilots from the NSFK for operations on the powered version of the aircraft. Known as the 'Spatz' (Sparrow), only one prototype was completed, seen here, which was flown on at least one occasion at the Reich Gliding School at Trebbin in March 1945

The first, tentative moves towards preparing the *Volksjäger* for war came in November 1944 when representatives of the NSFK (see Chapter One) visited Schwechat ostensibly to oversee the construction of a glider-trainer version of the He 162. Whilst there, they also discussed a glider training programme, presumably with the intention to prepare potential Hitler Youth fliers for graduation onto the jet fighter. On 17 November Francke noted that in consultation with the Luftwaffe's *General der Fliegerausbildung* (Commanding General of Flight Training), a powered trainer version of the He 162 was also to be considered. Curiously, it was agreed that the design should feature 'room for two men in the cockpit by lengthening the fuselage. Emergency exit for the second man will be through the cockpit floor'.

However, it seems that by February 1945 EHAG was experiencing problems in locating skilled labour for work on the two-seat glider, which was designated the He 162 S 'Spatz' (Sparrow). It is believed that some examples were built at Schönhagen, near Hannover, and a prototype was tested by Ing Haase on 28 March 1945. The aircraft flew without any problems. Based on this performance, it was proposed to build further examples that were to be towed into the air, and others with dummy engines and a fixed undercarriage.

Also in a revealing memo from November 1944, the armaments manufacturer Rheinmetall-Borsig, whose MK 108 30 mm cannon would be installed in a number of the He 162 prototypes, advised EHAG that such a weapon would allow the *Volksjäger* to effectively attack formations of Allied heavy bombers. When mounting such attacks, it was foreseen that the He 162 would approach from 1000 to 1500 m above and behind the bombers, then dive below the formation and pull up at an 80-degree angle, closing to between 600 and 800 m before opening fire. Fire was to cease when a 60-degree angle had been reached and the engagement broken off. 'We need to know the speed in such an attack', Francke noted, 'and duration of effective firing times when attacking B-17s and B-29s'. His reference to the American B-29 Superfortress is indicative of the belief held by the Germans that the USAAF would soon be operating its formidable new heavy bomber types over Europe.

Whilst there was little doubt that the Me 262 was a first-rate and technologically advanced interceptor, and would be able to meet the B-29 threat, output of the Messerschmitt was proving slow. What was needed to defend the Reich was a high-speed fighter able to be built quickly and cheaply. In late 1944 the He 162 offered a solution.

In late January 1945 Reichsmarschall Göring had replaced Generalleutnant Adolf Galland as the *General der Jagdflieger* (General of Fighters) following worsening disagreements, particularly over the deployment of the Me 262, with Oberst Gordon Gollob, a former *Kommodore* of JG 77 and the third recipient of the Diamonds to the Knight's Cross. Within days of his appointment, Gollob addressed a major staff conference in Berlin. The aim of the meeting, intriguingly, was to tackle 'the current personnel and materials situation with a view to avoiding the Reichsmarschall's suggestions that cannot be realised'.

Gollob wanted to achieve a smooth transition of two piston-engined fighter *Geschwader*, JG 300 and JG 301, which had been assigned to the Reich defence operations, over to the Me 262 in order to supplement the operations of JG 7, which was also equipped with the Messerschmitt interceptor. He also wanted to speed up the transition of former bomber units belonging to IX.(J) *Fliegerkorps* – KG(J) 54, III./KG(J) 6, KG(J) 55, KG(J) 27 and I. and II./KG(J) 6 – onto the jet fighter. Parallel to this was a plan to form a new *Jagdgeschwader*, JG 80, to train up on the He 162. However, this proposal was abandoned in the light of a downturn in production of the Fw 190. It was therefore proposed to cancel the planned establishment of I./JG 80 and to draw on existing Fw 190 units for conversion to the He 162. As a result, Gollob ordered the conversion of I./JG 1 to the *Volksjäger*.

On 11 February Gollob flew from Berlin to his native Vienna to inspect the He 162. That the *General der Jagdflieger* attached considerable importance to his visit is borne out by the fact that he was accompanied by a senior RLM engineer, Stabs Ingenieur Rauchensteiner, Oberstleutnant Walter Dahl, the 93-victory fighter ace and Knight's Cross-holder who had recently commanded JG 300 but who was now serving on Gollob's staff as *Inspekteur der Tagjäger* (Inspector of Day Fighters), Oberst Edgar Petersen, the *Kommandeur der Erprobungsstellen* and Hauptmann Horst Geyer from Gollob's staff.

The EHAG team invited Gollob and Rauchensteiner to fly the He 162 M3, which both officers duly did, and Gollob attained a speed

Oberst Gordon Gollob, a highly decorated 150-victory fighter ace, was appointed *General der Jagdflieger* in late January 1945. He became closely involved in the Luftwaffe's procurement of the He 162 and flew the type himself at Schwechat on 11 February 1945

of 650 km/h during his brief flight. After their flights both men opined that the He 162 was, without question, an excellent fighter aircraft. Gollob was informed, politely, that he was welcome to return to Vienna to fly the aircraft whenever he wished as long as he flew it within the recommended speed limits. At one point after his flight, Gollob remarked to the EHAG representatives that the *Führer* had been informed in a recent report that 30 He 162s were ready in Vienna for operations. However, according to the information he had to hand, as of 10 February there were no operational aircraft, and just four flyable, with a further 14 undergoing conversion and final assembly. Upon enquiring of Francke when these aircraft would be ready for operations, the response was the middle of April.

Gollob also stressed to Francke the need for the He 162 to be able to operate with RATO units. Indeed, the required runway and takeoff distance for the He 162 was the same as for the Me 262 due to the increased requirement for fuel and endurance, and thus its increase in weight. Gollob also agreed with the recommendations of Petersen and Geyer that the He 162 should be fitted with an ejector seat, which, if needed, would throw a pilot well clear of the jet engine located immediately behind his cockpit while travelling at high speeds. In addition, a strengthened metal frame for the cockpit hood and windscreen was to be investigated.

When it came to armament, Gollob was of the opinion that each of the He 162A-1's two MK 108 cannon should carry 80 rounds per gun rather than the proposed 60. EHAG advised that it would investigate the ramifications of the resulting increase in weight and the effect on the centre of gravity. However, events overtook this when Allied bombing of the Rheinmetall manufacturing plant halted supply of the MK 108, thus making the need for the installation of the MG 151 as an alternative (as fitted to the He 162A-2) an urgent priority. For his part, Gollob remained in favour of the MK 108, presumably because of experiences with the weapon in the Me 262, and took steps to investigate whether any other companies could manufacture the gun under license.

One encouraging development was that the long-awaited EZ 42 gyroscopic gunsight, designed to work with both the MK 108 and MG 151, was finally ready – it was envisaged that all series aircraft from 1 May 1945 were to be fitted with this sight. Finally, Gollob requested that the feasibility of fitting 55 mm R4M air-to-air rockets (planned for the Me 262) was also to be investigated by EHAG and findings reported to him by 20 February.

Following his visit to Vienna, Gollob ordered that trials with He 162 series models should commence at the *Erprobungsstelle* Rechlin from March 1945 on the basis that the first operational aircraft would become available from mid-April. The first operational *Gruppe* was to be ready from mid-May, with commencement of pilot and groundcrew training at the beginning of March.

Two weeks later, following Gollob's instructions, the Luftwaffe finally got its hands on the He 162. On 26 February a small detachment of ten pilots, formed into an *Auffangstaffel* (Collection Squadron) under the leadership of Oberleutnant August Hachtel of 2./JG 1, journeyed to Heidfeld with the objective of picking up He 162s as they came off the production lines. The *Staffel* was one of two such units that Gollob intended would accept and collect He 162s from Vienna, Marienehe and Bernburg.

In this regard, it was planned that 2./JG 1 would eventually transfer completely to Vienna, while 3./JG 1 would transfer to Marienehe and Bernburg. Additionally, Gollob wanted one *Staffel* from II./JG 1 to be sent to Vienna at the end of February. Until that time, the technical personnel from the allocated *Staffel* were to be instructed by groundcrew from EHAG using the prototypes so that the unit would be ready to take over the new aircraft when they were delivered. Gollob believed that it was important that personnel from II. *Gruppe* should be included as part of the test programme in order for them to obtain a good understanding of the machine well in advance, and to enable a mass transition to the He 162.

August Hachtel, who was born on 6 March 1916 in Stuttgart, was an extremely experienced airman. He had joined the Luftwaffe in November 1935, and on completion of pilot training in August 1939 was posted to *Stukageschwader* 7./StG 51 (later 4./StG 1). Apart from a brief spell with StG 3 in 1940, he remained with 4./StG 1 until November 1942. A very accomplished NCO ground-attack pilot, Hachtel was credited with the destruction of 32 enemy tanks and shipping totalling 32,000 tons. During the autumn of 1942 he flew 500 sorties over Russia and was awarded the Ritterkreuz on 6 January 1942, having also received the Ehrenpokal from Göring in September 1941 and the Deutsches Kreuz the following month.

From November 1942 until April 1944 Hachtel served as a flying instructor with the *Ergänzungsstaffel* StG 1 and 2./StG 103, during which time he was promoted to Leutnant in August 1943. He was then posted to *Erprobungskommando* 16 at Bad Zwischenahn in April 1944, where he was involved in trials using the Me 163 rocket-powered interceptor. In December 1944 he carried out experiments with the SG 500 '*Jägerfaust*' 30 mm automatic upward-firing weapon, but suffered severe back injuries and concussion on 24 December 1944 when the SG 500 installation in the Me 163B V45 in which he was flying fired prematurely. The shock from the muzzles of the barrels shattered the aircraft's canopy and Hachtel received a hard blow to his head. He managed to land the rocket fighter while still dazed and with the sun in his eyes, but the aircraft was 40 per cent damaged.

On 14 February 1945 *Erprobungskommando* 16 was disbanded at Brandis and Hachtel received orders to report to the EHAG works at Heidfeld to command the *Auffangstaffel*, and also to undergo familiarisation on the He 162. The decision to send Hachtel to Vienna may have been linked to Gollob's orders earlier in the month to the effect that the Me 163-equipped I. and II./JG 400 were to re-equip with the He 162 'later'. This seems to have been a revision of his directive of 30 January, in which it was stated that JG 400 was to retain the Me 163 and then make the transition to the planned Me 263.

As his right-hand man, Hachtel was accompanied by another experienced airman, Oberfeldwebel Friedrich Oeltjen. Born on 7 April 1913 in Astederfeld, Oldenburg, Oeltjen started his flying career in 1937 at the controls of transport gliders. A year later he underwent training at the A/B flying school in Magdeburg and in 1939 he was posted to JG 54. From 1941 to 1943 he served as an instructor at the *Jagdfliegerschule* at Zerbst, afterwards returning to JG 54. In September 1943 Oeltjen was

Oberleutnant August Hachtel spent a frustrating few weeks in early 1945 as leader of the first Luftwaffe *Auffangstaffel* intended to take on the He 162. An extremely experienced dive-bomber and ground-attack pilot, prior to becoming involved with the He 162 programme, Hachtel had previously flown the Me 163 rocket-powered interceptor fitted with special armament

He 162 M23 (A-2) Wk-Nr 220006 'VI+IP' photographed in a sorry state at Munich-Riem after the war. The aircraft lacks its nosewheel, and later its engine was also removed. The M23 was first flown on 19 March 1945 with Gerhard Gleuwitz at the controls

posted to *Erprobungskommando* 16, and he remained with the unit until it was disbanded. Awarded the Iron Cross First Class and *Frontflug-Spange* in Silver, he made a total of 58 sharp takeoffs in the Me 163B, but did not fly any operational sorties in the rocket fighter.

The Heinkel technicians reported that when the Luftwaffe pilots arrived at Heidfeld, 'these men were incredibly impatient to take on the He 162s that had been cleared by our technicians. As soon as they were ready, the pilots took over the aircraft'. It seems the memories of the EHAG men may have been cloudy, however, for when Hachtel and his unit arrived at Heidfeld expecting to take delivery of the first He 162s, they were to be disappointed. Despite the Luftwaffe's enthusiasm to take on the He 162s, things moved very slowly while EHAG continued to grapple with the prototype development programme. Eventually, a solitary machine, He 162 M19 A-02 Wk-Nr 220002 'VI+IL', was handed over to Hachtel, but the *Auffangstaffel* was ordered not to fly the aircraft at speeds in excess of 500 km/h, above 3000 m and for longer than 15 minutes.

By mid-March, however, Hachtel had telexed Gollob to advise that eight pilots had completed their conversion courses, but that no ground personnel had arrived for training. Nevertheless, despite Hachtel's best endeavours, a dark shadow began to fall across the detachment's activities. On 4 March He 162 M22 A-05 Wk-Nr 220005 'VI+IO' suffered 15 per cent damage during a test flight – with Feldwebel Denzin at the controls – to check wing root strength. On the 9th the engine of an unidentified Heinkel that Denzin was flying, and in which he had attained a speed of 955 km/h, cut out upon landing.

Three days later, Feldwebel Wanke miraculously escaped with his life when the engine of He 162 M8 Wk-Nr 200008 'VI+IH' suddenly stopped functioning and the aircraft somersaulted just short of the runway and caught fire. The same day, during landing, Feldwebel Gleuwitz badly damaged He 162 M26 Wk-Nr 220009 'VI+IS'. On 14 March another aircraft was destroyed when Unteroffizier Tautz of 2./JG 1, having aborted a first attempt to land in He 162 M19, made another circuit and then hit a pile of barrels on the runway. M19 somersaulted and caught fire, while Tautz, who was making his first flight in the *Volksjäger*, was thrown out of the cockpit and killed. It was thought pilot error was the cause of the accident. This aircraft had been intended to test a 20-degree V-tail in comparison flights with M3.

Francke remained undaunted by these initial setbacks to the trials, writing in a memo that month, 'When the He 162 is finally ready, then it will become the most economic aircraft in Germany in terms of material used and will be much sought after. No one else will be able to do this'. That may have been his opinion, but the Luftwaffe's pilots viewed the He 162 with a mixture of wonderment and apprehension. The cockpit at least seemed well laid out, as Oberleutnant Wolfgang Wollenweber of 3./JG 1 recalled;

'Located immediately behind the nose cone, the cockpit's large, cleanly moulded Plexiglas canopy promised excellent forward and lateral visibility, the instruments had been reduced to a bare minimum and were clearly laid out and the pilot had even been provided with an ejection seat.'

Wollenweber, a veteran pilot who had flown Bf 110s with 13.(Z)/JG 5 in the far north, also remembered being briefed by Heinkel works pilot Flugkapitän Heinrich, who advised a group of Luftwaffe pilots that although there would be no training version of the He 162, 'You *will* be given a set of pilot's handling notes. These you will have to read and learn thoroughly. You will also receive instructions on the ground. One of our works pilots will explain all the controls to you. He will show you how to handle the throttle, and point out which instruments you need to keep a special eye on. He'll talk you through what you have to do at takeoff, after lift-off, while in the air, and when landing. When the He 162 is demonstrated, fix firmly in your minds the exact point of lift-off, watch how the pilot handles the approach when he comes back in, and note precisely where he touches down'.

Upon seating himself in the cockpit of the Heinkel, the hood would be dropped down above the pilot's head and an overhead catch fastened. The pilot was presented with four groups of instruments – for the engine, for flying, for the thrust nozzle and various control switches. Looking directly forward, there was a main panel containing the turn-and-bank indicator, airspeed indicator, climb/descent indicator, compass, oil pressure, jet pipe temperature and fuel gauges, rev counter and oxygen gauge. To his left against the cockpit wall were the RATO switch, fuel cock, throttle, undercarriage control, rudder and elevator trim controls and flap manual control pump, while on a control panel to his right were the control box of the FuG 24 R/T and FuG 25a IFF transponder, starter switch and the electrics console. Above the main instrument panel was mounted the Revi gunsight, and below the panel was a window to check on the nosewheel retraction. The trigger for the ejection seat was located to the right of the seat between the seat handle and the frame of the seat.

The BMW 003 engine could be started with an outboard battery.

The ejector seat for the He 162. The release trigger can be seen fitted to the side of the bucket seat. Behind the upright was a hollow piston to which was fitted a cartridge and firing pin that detonated when the pilot pulled the trigger

The instrument panel of He 162A-2 Wk-Nr 120095 'White 20' of JG 1 at Leck in May 1945. Instrumentation on the top row from left includes turn and bank indicator, airspeed indicator, turbine temperature and rpm. Lower row, again from left to right, includes hand pump, homing gauge, altimeter, compass, fuel pressure and fuel gauge, ammunition counters and oxygen pressure indicator. Immediately below the instrument panel is the glass observation window used to monitor nosewheel retraction

The pilot would turn on the thrust nozzle, gauge system, starter and fuel pump and then use the Riedel starter switch. At 1100 rpm he would operate the ignition and priming for the jet unit using a button on the control column. At between 1800 and 2000 rpm, he would release the Riedel switch and at 3000 rpm the pilot would move the throttle to its ground-idling notch. He would then warm the engine up by running it at 4000-5000 rpm for two to three minutes. For a trial run on the ground, the thrust nozzle was switched to 'S' ('Start') for high-speed flight at an altitude of 4000-8000 m at 6000 rpm. Then the throttle was advanced smoothly to its last notch, with the engine running at 9500 rpm.

To prepare for flight, the brakes were kept on and the undercarriage lever in the down position, while the turbines were started and run up for three minutes and the revs were checked at full power. The engine was then throttled back and the brakes released, at which point the pilot would taxi the aircraft out using the brakes gently. He lined up with the runway, applied the brakes, swiftly checked the cockpit instrumentation and controls, checked the trim and set the nozzle for climb and high-speed flight over 8 km. The pilot also pumped the flaps down until the wing trailing edges were clearly visible. At the point of takeoff the throttle was opened up to about 6000 rpm against the brakes, then released, before slowly opening back up to full throttle. The aircraft would leave the ground at around 200 km/h and speed would be increased to 300 km/h before entering a climb at the same speed. Then the undercarriage was pulled up.

Pilots were warned that the controls were very light, and that the aircraft could occasionally be unstable about the vertical axis. When the fuel gauge showed 300 litres, flight was to be ended. For landing, speed was reduced to 350 km/h, at which point the gear was lowered. The pilot would pump down the flaps by hand, which required considerable force and time. Speed was reduced to around 200-250 km/h, and the angle of approach was adjusted so that the turbine was still running at around 6000 rpm. The throttle was closed ten seconds before the anticipated landing. Once down, brakes were to be used as sparingly as possible. Because of the length of time required to open the throttle (around ten seconds), any overshoot action had to be taken very early.

The pilot would then throttle down to the ground-idling notch and switch the thrust nozzle to 'A' for starting, taxiing and idling. He then throttled down to a stop and set the fuel cut-off, pumps and battery to off.

In early February Reichsmarschall Göring ordered that I./JG 1 should relocate from Garz, on the island of Usedom, to Parchim, 70 km south of Rostock, 'for training and re-equipment with the He 162'. Shortly afterwards a small group of pilots from the *Gruppe* under Leutnant Karl-Emil Demuth travelled from Parchim to the Heinkel works at Rostock-Marienehe effectively as another ad hoc *Auffangstaffel*.

Demuth would be closely involved with the He 162's operational service. Born on 22 December 1916 in Affaltrach, near Heilbronn, his Luftwaffe service had commenced on 29 October 1935 when he joined 4./*Flieger Ersatz Abteilung* 15 in Neubiburg for basic service training, followed by preliminary flight training with *Fliegerausbildungsregiment* 23 at Kaufbeuren from 1 November 1938 to 3 September 1939. After a short spell at the *Fluglehrerschule der Luftwaffe* at Brandenburg-Briest through to the end of November 1939, Demuth returned to Kaufbeuren as a flying instructor, where he remained until 18 August 1942.

Demuth then served for a year with the *Luftkriegschule* 2 at Werder/Havel, during which time he spent six weeks on the Eastern Front flying supply missions in an old Junkers W 34 from Warsaw to Dnjepopetrowsk, as well as embarking upon supply missions to trapped German forces at Stalingrad. He subsequently joined 2./JG 102, with whom he learned to fly the Bf 109. Via a short spell at 3./*Jagdgruppe West* at Casseau, in France, Demuth joined 3./JG 1 on 19 August 1943 at Deelen, in Holland, and remained with the unit from that point on. Karl-Emil Demuth was credited with 16 aerial victories, all scored in the West and all thought to be USAAF aircraft.

Demuth and his group waited in vain for any He 162s at Rostock, as production there was still slow. Eventually, he decided to head south with a handful of pilots to Vienna – a difficult enough undertaking in itself by that stage of the war. He arrived there on 4 March to be greeted with the deflating news that he and his men would have to share the only available aircraft, M19, with Hachtel's group, although more machines were promised. Furthermore, there were strict airspeed and flight-time restrictions imposed. After witnessing the fatal crash of Unteroffizier Tautz on the 14th, however, a dispirited Demuth decided to head back north to Parchim to await further developments. So much for any intended familiarisation on the *Volksjäger*.

In the meantime, as planned, a third group of pilots, this time from 3./JG 1, was despatched to Rostock-Marienehe in late March. These airmen enjoyed the rare luxury of being accommodated in a resort hotel in Warnemünde, on the Baltic coast, while awaiting their opportunity to fly the He 162. Wolfgang Wollenweber recalled being taken into one of only three assembly halls that had not been damaged by bombs;

'When we entered the hangar-like shed we saw a row of machines all carefully covered by tarpaulins. When the tarpaulins were removed, our group's reactions were mixed. Faces at first reflected surprise, and then either enthusiasm or scepticism. My initial thought was that if that clumsy, almost misshapen great lump of a turbine hadn't been stuck on top of its neat little fuselage, this could have been the most beautiful and elegant aircraft I had ever clapped eyes on. I was also hugely impressed by the manner in which the most basic of materials had been combined with such a revolutionary concept.'

Eventually, at the end of the month, some of the pilots were able to make flights of between ten and 20 minutes duration. Leutnant Hans Berger recalled;

'We viewed this little aircraft, with its wooden wings and large turbine on its back behind the cockpit, with a degree of scepticism. Accustomed to the protection of the Fw 190's massive engine, we felt exposed and unprotected behind the thin leaf of the cockpit Plexiglas. Even more importantly, there were several weaknesses that caused us concern, such as the fragile join between the wings and the fuselage. In flight, you had to pilot it with an incredible sensitivity, because the aircraft reacted to even the smallest touch on the stick – she was that soft. It was especially at low speeds that the aircraft became most dangerous for it skidded easily. Once again, and even

In early February 1945 Leutnant Karl-Emil Demuth (right), an experienced military aviator, led a small group of pilots from JG 1 to the EHAG factory at Rostock-Marienehe with the intention of collecting some of the first He 162s for the *Geschwader*. He was to be disappointed. Demuth is seen here in the autumn of 1944 with Leutnant Gottfried Just of I./JG 1, who was killed in action over the Ardennes on 27 December 1944

more so than in the past, the lack of training amongst the new pilots was evident. With a machine so sensitive, intuitive flying was vital.

'In order to start the engine, it was necessary to use an electric starter coupled to the turbine by pressing on a red button. There was a loud noise often accompanied by a jet of small, spitting flames. But if the noise was loud outside the aircraft, one was aware of it only slightly in the cockpit, and even less so after takeoff. You couldn't hear the slipstream, just as with a glider. The most impressive thing without doubt was the speed – 750, 800, 850, 900 km/h. I remember several exciting flights where I reached nearly 1000 km/h at low altitude over the sandy beaches above the island of Amrum. The short range was the only handicap – 35 to 40 minutes flying duration at high altitude, and by drastic economy you could stretch it to 50 minutes. If you encountered the enemy, the order was to attack from a more elevated position. We regretted the lack of opportunities to measure our new aircraft against enemy fighters.'

In Vienna, Leutnant Hachtel remained unimpressed with the He 162. He believed that its limited endurance needed to be increased by 40 minutes for the aircraft to have any purposeful combat capability. He was also becoming increasingly frustrated with what seemed a lack of any real progress on the part of EHAG, as there was still little sign of the aircraft being available in meaningful numbers. He informed Francke that he would return to Berlin to advise the OKL on the state of affairs in Vienna, but it seems Francke dissuaded him. It is possible that Francke told Hachtel of the new delivery plan for the series aircraft, namely that the first five machines would go to his *Auffangstaffel*, the following eight jets would be allocated to an *Erprobungskommando* at Lechfeld and a further seven He 162s to another *Erprobungskommando* at Rechlin-Roggenthin.

On 26 March, however, much to Hachtel's continuing dismay, orders came through that all completed He 162s were to be used for test purposes only. The same day, new orders were issued by OKL relocating the *Gruppen* of JG 1 in readiness for the first He 162s arriving off the production lines at Junkers Bernburg (23 March) and EHAG Oranienburg and Rostock (24 and 25 March, respectively). *Stab* and I./JG 1 were to relocate to Köthen, II./JG 1 to Vienna-Schwechat and III./JG 1 to Lüneberg.

In accordance with this, on 23 March a detachment of ten pilots from JG 1 under Oberleutnant Wollenweber had been ordered to transfer to Bernburg, where they would take delivery of He 162s and then transfer on to Lechfeld. This detachment left Parchim and travelled through the night to Bernburg, 230 km away, in a small truck and two trailers in order to avoid enemy air attack. Each man carried only one item of baggage – all that it was possible to accommodate behind the seat of an He 162. Wollenweber and his men arrived at the Bernburg works in the early hours of the morning. After 'hammering on the gates for some time' they were eventually let in by a blind, half-asleep civilian night watchman. At daylight the next morning, the Luftwaffe pilots made their own tour of the works, but found the assembly halls locked. Then, over breakfast, an engineer broke the news to them that no *Volksjäger* were ready for them and that it would be some time before they would be.

On the morning of the 26th, an engineer arrived at Bernburg from the *Erprobungsstelle* at Rechlin, bringing orders for Wollenweber to transfer

no fewer than 15 He 162s not to Parchim, but to Lechfeld, making an interim stop at Unterschlauersbach. Wollenweber recalled;

'Dumbfounded, I asked how on earth we were supposed to fly 15 machines to Bavaria with just ten pilots. He could do no more than shrug helplessly, but he did say we would be getting two of the works' own test pilots.'

When Wollenweber attempted to express his concerns about his new orders by telephone to a senior officer at the RLM, he was subjected to a violent tirade and threatened with court-martial if he disobeyed. The following afternoon the pilots went out onto the airfield, where they were introduced to Flugkapitän Hermann Steckhan, who was planning to take He 162 Wk-Nr 310001 aloft on a demonstration flight for the Luftwaffe pilots. They would be able to listen in to the works pilot's in-flight R/T communication with the ground controllers. Steckhan recorded in the subsequent report;

'On 27 March at 1658 hrs I took off in He 162 "1" on an acceptance flight. The takeoff went smoothly. The machine lifted off quite quickly. At the edge of the airfield the engine suddenly began to vibrate. Fuel pressure fell slowly. I switched the undercarriage from "up" at which the gear unlocked. I closed the fuel cock and then drew to an abrupt stop. After a moment I came around and recovered from the shock.'

Steckhan's report is one of considerable understatement, and conceals the drama of the event. Indeed, as Wollenweber remembered, 'At a height of just 150 metres the turbine abruptly cut out. We heard Steckhan calmly report that he was doing 240 km/h and was having problems with the automatic thrust nozzle control settings. After completing half a circuit he came in at 50 metres for a deadstick landing. This was much too high, and he had too much speed. We watched as the tiny machine smashed down hard onto the runway. The turbine was ripped off upon impact and went sailing off to the right. The two wooden wings snapped off, the cockpit was squashed flat and the fuselage broke into several pieces. It was little short of a miracle that Steckhan was able to extricate himself from the machine. He managed to stagger for a few paces, but then collapsed in a heap'.

Steckhan had suffered severe facial and body injuries. At this, the Luftwaffe pilots voiced their misgivings at being made to fly such an aircraft. Nevertheless, after a period of bad weather and further delays in production, finally on 31 March an impatient yet apprehensive

Flugkapitän Hermann Steckhan (far left) prepares for a flight in He 162 Wk-Nr 310001. On 27 March 1945, Steckhan planned to fly a demonstration flight in the aircraft for pilots of JG 1 over Bernburg, but the Heinkel crashed upside down shortly after takeoff, its wings and engine breaking off and its cockpit being crushed. Somehow, Steckhan survived

Wollenweber braved his first test flight in He 162 Wk-Nr 310006. He found himself reacting positively to the experience;

'I went down low and thundered across the rooftops of Bernburg at 800 km/h. I was filled with elation. I would never have believed that the He 162 could be flown so easily, and at speeds that no enemy fighter could possibly match. With this little beauty we need no longer worry about what sort of opposition we were up against. All they would see of us would be our backsides as we shot past them. And if we did run into trouble, we could always use our superior speed to climb or dive away.'

Once safely back on the ground, however, Wollenweber was careful to warn his group about the excess use of rudder and the resulting slipping and skidding, and the careful use of the controls needed on takeoff. The rudder problem was one of several shortcomings identified by Oberst Edgar Petersen, the *Kommandeur der Erprobungsstellen*, following an assessment at Rechlin of machines built by Junkers. In addition, Petersen noted, maximum speed was 100 km/h less than that promised, endurance was never more than 30 minutes and the altitude performance of the BMW 003 engine apparently precluded any attempt to discover the true ceiling performance of the aircraft. Furthermore, the engine could not deliver its full thrust, the nosewheel was too weak, the wing fuel tank leaked, acceleration interfered with the fuel feed and generally the flying qualities were poor, especially in rolls.

Eventually, on 1 April, Wollenweber selected three of his pilots to transfer the first Heinkels to Lechfeld, with Leutnant Büttner piloting He 162 Wk-Nr 310006, Feldwebel Strauss in Wk-Nr 310002 and Unteroffizier Dobrath in Wk-Nr 310018. Strauss made it to Lechfeld but his aircraft crashed on landing and was destroyed. He suffered a fractured skull and burns. Dobrath made it to Unterschlauersbach, only to discover that he was not able to land there because the airfield had fallen to the Americans. He was thus forced to make an emergency landing, out of fuel, in open countryside east of Nürnberg. He eventually managed to return to Bernburg by means of train and hitching lifts. Büttner disappeared en route.

At Lechfeld, Wollenweber's men were to report to a newly formed '*Einsatzerprobungskommando* He 162', which was supposedly being organised under the command of Oberstleutnant Heinz Bär. In reality, Bär, one of the Jagdwaffe's most experienced and accomplished combat pilots who had been appointed commander of the Me 262 training unit III./EJG 2 in mid-February, had essentially become 'overseer' at Lechfeld, with umbrella responsibility for a range of tactical and technical training. Quite frankly, the Me 262 was his priority – the He 162 was not. It is unlikely that Bär took little more than a passing, and at most, curious interest in the He 162.

All this became academic, for on 11 April the decision was taken to evacuate Bernburg in the face of the Soviet advance. 'The place was like a disturbed ants' nest', Wollenweber recorded. 'Machines were being pushed out of the sheds and fuelled up, people were running about with boxes and cartons stuffed with blueprints and documents, smoke was curling into the air all over the field as factory records were burned in empty oil drums'. The day before he had made an '*Aufklärung*' (a 'reconnaissance') for 35 minutes in He 162 Wk-Nr 210011, having taken off from Bernburg in the early afternoon. He noted in his logbook, 'Nordhausen, Mühlhausen. Flak over Langensalza airfield'.

Wollenweber and his remaining pilots were hurriedly ordered to fly six He 162s to Ludwigslust, from where they would hopefully join the rest of JG 1. On 8 April a heavy USAAF bombing raid had left the runway at Parchim unusable, hence the choice of Ludwigslust. Taking off from Bernburg at 1755 hrs, five of the six aircraft, flown by Wollenweber, Oberfähnrich Stenschke, Oberfähnrich Köttgen, Unteroffizier Hartung and Unteroffizier Riemer, made it to their destination, but one machine, flown by Fähnrich Franz Mann of 3./JG 1, flew to Salzwedel instead, where it brushed the tops of some trees as the pilot attempted to land there. The Heinkel was seen to bank steeply, trailing white smoke, before it crashed into the ground and caught fire, with Mann believed to have been killed.

On 12 April Junkers test pilot Heinrich Osterwald flew Wk-Nr 310021 out of Bernburg to Ludwigslust – a flight that took 20 minutes. Altogether, Junkers at Bernburg is believed to have produced 15 He 162s.

Meanwhile, on 27 March, OKL and the *General der Jagdflieger* had optimistically forecast that 2./JG 1 would receive 18 He 162s based on the projected deliveries from Junkers, with a further seven machines expected to arrive from Languste. The following day at Schwechat, August Hachtel received a telex informing him that He 162s were to be accepted from EHAG only if the BMW engines had been converted to accept J2 fuel. Hachtel was also told to prepare seven aircraft, as and when they became available, for transfer to Lechfeld for flight-testing, presumably by Wollenweber's expected detachment.

By the 30th no aircraft had been delivered to either Lechfeld or the E-Stelle Rechlin, which was also awaiting them. That day, however, Hachtel signalled Gollob that he was in a position to begin ferrying aircraft from Schwechat to Lechfeld 'in a few days'. According to Hachtel, 'the pilots need a few more practise takeoffs before then. The pilots must return by aircraft'. He added, 'I request immediate information'.

However, by the time the first He 162s did eventually reach the Luftwaffe in the south, Hachtel was not at all impressed, since the fighter's performance was way below the widely promoted expectations. He had left Vienna by 11 April and would play no further part in subsequent developments with the *Volksjäger*. What remained of his detachment at Heidfeld from 2./JG 1 was ordered to transfer as *Stabsstaffel* JG 1 to Lechfeld (and/or Memmingen) for operations as part of '*Erprobungskommando* Lechfeld'.

The situation in the Vienna area had become as bad as that at Bernburg. Following authorisation from Hauptdienstleiter Saur on 31 March, the Heinkel works was evacuated in the face of the threatening Soviet advance from the east. The He 162 M11 (fitted with a Jumo 004 engine) had been destroyed by bombing at Languste, while the M9 and M10 were blown up to prevent capture by the Russians. Ten aircraft had been flown out of Schwechat and Heidfeld by the end of March via Langenlebarn and Hörsching to Lechfeld. One He 162 was abandoned at Hörsching during the transfer, and another was destroyed when it crashed and overturned not far from Langenlebarn during the leg from Munich to Lechfeld, killing its pilot, Leutnant Kemnitz.

At around the same time a specially requisitioned train carrying Francke, Günter and approximately 35 key members of staff departed Vienna bound for Gandersheim, in the Harz Mountains. However, due to the American advance from the west, the party had to divert to the small Heinkel satellite facility at Jenbach, in the Tyrol. Karl Frydag later recalled;

'On 1 April 1945 our workshop in Vienna had to close down. Complete machines were conveyed, with larger fittings ready to be mounted at the Amme-Luther-Seck Werk being transferred as far as possible. Drawings and documents were secured and transported to Jenbach, where they were hidden in a cellar near the Achensee to protect them from being destroyed. At Rostock, meanwhile, production had begun with similar difficulties. The last news came from Rostock at the beginning of April. Then every communication ceased. From mid-April, communications were also lost with Junkers at Dessau. By the time we had to leave Vienna, about 12 complete aircraft were ready there. They were to be flown to Hörsching, near Linz, and to Lechfeld, but as we later heard, not all of them arrived.'

Of the Vienna facilities, EHAG Süd at Schwechat turned out approximately eight aircraft while EHAG at Hinterbrühl (Languste) produced 20. By the end of April, production of the He 162 had all but ceased at EHAG's plant at Rostock-Marienehe due to the rapid advance of the Soviet Army, and on 2 May Rostock fell to the Russians.

It is believed that a total of 171 He 162s were manufactured in total, with Luftwaffe delivery statistics listing 116 Heinkels as being delivered by the various factories. Only 56 of these aircraft made it to the Luftwaffe, however. EHAG Nord at Rostock-Marienehe and Theresienfeld produced approximately 55 aircraft, while ten were delivered by the infamous Mittelwerke underground slave labour factory at Nordhausen and the Deutsche Lufthansa facility at Oranienburg. Despite the chaos of the closing months of the war, EHAG's remarkable contribution to military aviation history produced – in just six months – the first operationally ready single-engined jet fighter, and the first of its kind to incorporate an ejection seat.

One of the entrances to the notorious cave factory at Nordhausen in the Harz Mountains known as the 'Mittelwerke'. EHAG could draw upon a force of 7000 malnourished slave labourers working in airless, poorly lit, cramped, noisy and dirty conditions at Nordhausen to help build the He 162, with an estimated 300 man-hours needed to produce each machine

CHAPTER FOUR

JAGDGESCHWADER 1

Before the formation of the *Auffangstaffeln* mentioned in the previous chapter, it had been decided to form an *Erprobungskommando* with which to assess the He 162 while Generalleutnant Galland was still in office as *General der Jagdflieger*. One of Galland's last orders before being replaced by Oberst Gollob was for the establishment of a new *Gruppe* comprising three *Staffeln* (each with 12 aircraft), together with a *Gruppenstab* (of four aircraft), to be formed specifically to assess the He 162 as an operational aircraft. As in the style of other such units, it was to be known as *Erprobungskommando* 162. The Luftwaffe hoped that it would exist for no more than six months, by which time the aircraft would have proved itself.

During this evaluation period a new *Jagdgeschwader* was to be formed or another established *Gruppe* or *Geschwader* converted to specifically operate the *Volksjäger*. The plan was to base the *Kommando* either at, or as near to, the *Erprobungsstelle* at Rechlin as possible, the airfield at Lärz being seen as a likely site. The *E-Stelle* was notified formally of this proposal on 1 January 1945, with the official establishment order being issued to Oberst Petersen, the commander of the Rechlin station, on 9 January By this stage, however, Galland had been superseded as *General der Jagdflieger* by Gollob.

To oversee the formation of *Erprobungskommando* 162, and probably on Petersen's suggestion, the RLM appointed Hauptmann Horst Geyer –

The diminutive size of the He 162, together with its Lippisch-designed wingtips and slanting tail fins, are shown clearly in this view of what is believed to be 'White 21'. One member of the groundcrew is about to pull down the canopy, behind which can be seen a red and white engine intake cover which is marked with a '21'. The aircraft's nose has been finished in the national military colours of red, white and black, together with red arrows on either side. A generator cart is visible to the left of the photograph

formerly commander of *Erprobungskommando* 25 (a weapons evaluation unit specialising in devising means of attacking multi-engined bombers). Geyer's involvement seems to have been brief, however, with his activity being limited to ordering the transfer of 26 pilots to EHAG at Rostock-Marienehe for training and familiarisation purposes under the command of Oberleutnant Gert van Helden, formerly the technical officer in *Erprobungskommando* 262 and the adjutant of III./EJG 2. This group arrived at Rostock on 15 January, with a further four men joining them on the 18th.

Only a few days later, however, Gollob issued new instructions in which he cancelled the establishment of *Erprobungskommando* 162 in favour of a new *Gruppe*, to be known as I./JG 200, together with a *Stabsstaffel*. The *Gruppe* was to have a strength of 40 aircraft, with groundcrews being sourced from the embryonic II./JG 7, which, ironically, had previously been intended to equip with the Me 262 under the command of the sacked Generalleutnant Galland. This instruction was dropped in favour of a new designation, I./JG 80, but even this was changed on 29 January 1945 when Gollob decided to cancel it and instead convert the existing fighter *Gruppe* I./JG 1 to the He 162. Gollob's changes and his reasoning hinged on the fact that production of Fw 190 fighters was declining. 'Therefore', he wrote on the 30th, 'it should be possible to convert Fw 190 units to the He 162'.

I./JG 1 had been at the forefront of the *Reichsverteidigung* (air defence of the Reich) since 1942. In addition, the *Gruppe* had been one of those hurriedly rushed to France following the Allied invasion in June 1944, where its Fw 190A-8s had been outnumbered and mauled by overwhelming opposition. The unit's strength in pilots and aircraft had been severely depleted, and when it was posted back to Germany in the autumn of 1944, effectively, the *Gruppe* went under a reformation. The gaps in the ranks were filled by youthful replacement pilots with little training – one officer of the *Gruppe* recalled that they were 'little more than boys with only a few hours' flying time', while a pilot of 3. *Staffel* remembered how, by this time, 'everything had changed. Most of my comrades had disappeared. Some had been posted to other units, but the great majority had been killed in action. I could feel that the mood had changed'.

At the beginning of 1945, I./JG 1 was among those fighter *Gruppen* assigned to take part in Operation *Bodenplatte*, the massed, surprise fighter attack launched by the Luftwaffe against Allied tactical airfields across France, Belgium and Holland on New Year's Day. The *Gruppe* had had 13 Fw 190s destroyed and nine pilots lost in the operation, representing an unacceptably high 56 per cent loss rate in aircraft and a 39 per cent loss rate in pilots. Among the latter was the *Gruppenkommandeur*, Hauptmann Georg Hackbarth. His successor was a former bomber pilot, Major Günther Capito, who took command of the *Gruppe* at Twente, in Holland, although the *Geschwaderkommodore*, the highly decorated, illustrious and authoritarian fighter ace Oberstleutnant Herbert Ihlefeld, issued orders to the effect that command of I./JG 1 in the air would be assumed by the *Staffelkapitän* of 3. *Staffel*, Leutnant Karl-Emil Demuth (see Chapter Three). This measure was more to do with Capito's lack of fighter experience than any reflection of his command capabilities.

Despite his cheerful smile in this photograph, Oberstleutnant Herbert Ihlefeld, the *Kommodore* of JG 1, is remembered by several former He 162 pilots as a disciplined and authoritarian figure. Although he did not involve himself directly to any great extent in the day-to-day operations of the He 162, Ihlefeld kept a close eye on his charges' activities. A highly capable pilot and leader, Ihlefeld had previously commanded JG 52 and JG 11, as well as fighter training units. He is credited with 130 victories and was a recipient of the Knight's Cross with Oakleaves and Swords

In mid-January 1945 I./JG 1 departed Holland, having been ordered to relocate to the east, where it was to conduct ground-attack sorties and to provide fighter cover to convoys on the Baltic Sea engaged in evacuating the isolated forces of Army Group North from the Kurland pocket. However, only three weeks later, on 6 February, no less a figure than Reichsmarschall Göring instructed that I./JG 1 was to leave its base at Garz and transfer west to Parchim, via Anklam and Neubrandenburg, where it was to commence training and re-equipping with the He 162. The unit was to hand over its 23 Fw 190s to II./JG 1, which would deploy them in ground-attack operations against Soviet forces.

I./JG 1 duly departed Garz on 8 February in a convoy of 65 vehicles – a sight which would have proved tempting to any prowling Allied or Soviet aircraft. The *Gruppe* arrived at Parchim in the early hours of the 9th, having managed to evade bombing raids along the way. At Parchim the immediate lack of any Heinkels meant that training could be only theoretical, and this was delivered by a group of technicians and test pilots from EHAG Nord at Rostock.

As has been related in the previous chapter, when it seemed as if there would be no operationally ready He 162s appearing from Rostock for some time, Leutnant Demuth left Parchim to travel to Vienna in order to ascertain if any aircraft could be located there. He would not return north until mid-March. On 26 March, the *Geschwaderstab* and I./JG 1 were ordered to relocate south to Köthen, lying conveniently between the Junkers plant at Bernburg and the company's main works at Dessau.

In the meantime, the air war over Germany had taken on a grim cycle as the Jagdwaffe fought as best it could to defend the homeland against the formidable heavy bomber formations, hundreds strong, of the USAAF Eighth and Fifteenth Air Forces, as well as those of RAF Bomber Command, together with their ever-increasing numbers of escort fighters. At the end of March the heavy bombers targeted the U-boat pens, shipyards and oil storage tanks of the north German ports, as well as oil refineries at Zeitz and Bad Berka and other targets at Brandenburg, Gotha, Stendal, Salzwedel, Braunschweig and Halle.

Against such a situation, or perhaps because of it, on 31 March I./JG 1 received orders to prepare to transfer from Köthen to Leck airfield in far northern Germany, close to the Danish border, staging via Parchim and Ludwigslust. At some point the *Gruppe* had taken delivery of a handful of *Volksjäger*, for whilst briefly back at Parchim on the evening of the 31st Leutnant Berger of 3./JG 1 took He 162 'White 1' aloft for a 12-minute flight. Former transport pilot Hauptmann Heinz Künnecke, who was, ostensibly at least, the *Kapitän* of 1./JG 1, also made two airfield circuit flights of 15 and six minutes duration, respectively, in an unknown He 162 during the late afternoon. Künnecke had transitioned from flying transports with 4./TG 30 to fighters, serving with I./JG 103 and 15./EJG 1 before moving to JG 1.

Leutnant Gerhard Hanf also flew an unidentified He 162 for the first time the same evening;

'On 31 March 1945 I took off at 1830 hrs on my first flight from the airfield at Parchim. Before takeoff I was informed that performance was not to exceed 600 km/h, as there was a danger of a break-up in the air.

Leutnant Gerhard Hanf, photographed while serving with III./JG 77 in Rumania in 1943 shortly after having claimed a P-38 shot down for his second aerial victory. He became a member of II./JG 1 in August 1944 following his unit's reorganisation and first flew the He 162 in March 1945. Hanf made several flights from Leck, all without event, and from which he returned safely on each occasion

Five pilots of 3./JG 1 relax at their dispersal in 1945. Second from right is Fahnenjunker-Feldwebel Günther Kirchner, who first flew the He 162 on 4 April 1945. He would be killed two weeks later when he attempted to eject from his Heinkel after being attacked by enemy fighters over Leck airfield. Also in this photograph, second from left, is Feldwebel Rolf Ackermann, who lost his life a few days after Kirchner when his He 162 crashed at Leck

Not surprisingly, that was not much of a recommendation for the aircraft. Of course, prior to takeoff, I had no idea of the performance of the engine. Fully loaded, the machine took a long time to take off, but finally at 180 km/h it lifted off. The takeoff distance was at least double that of an Fw 190. In flight, the machine demonstrated good characteristics, and the rudders reacted very precisely to pressure. However, the controls were very basic. Following a quick half hour, my first flight ended without incident.'

Hanf had served with 4./JG 1 since that *Staffel* had evolved from 9./JG 77 in August 1944. Born on 16 May 1924, Hanf had joined the Luftwaffe in December 1941, graduating from *Luftkriegschule* 5 in Breslau to train as a fighter pilot with 2./JG 102, *Jagdfliegerschule* 2 and 2./Erg.JGr. Ost in 1942-43. In June 1943, he was promoted to Leutnant and assigned to III./JG 77, which was then operating over Italy and Rumania. Hanf saw combat with the unit in the Bf 109G-6, claiming two victories. In August 1944 he acted as *Staffelführer* and was awarded the Frontflug-Spange in Silver in September. Fighting over Normandy and the Western Front with JG 1 in Fw 190s from June 1944, Hanf claimed two P-47s shot down and also accounted for a tank destroyed in France in early August.

On 20 March the OKL had issued its orders for the wholesale conversion of JG 1 onto the He 162. This would see the *Stabsstaffel* established with a strength of 16 He 162s and I./JG 1 operating 52 *Volksjäger*, while II./JG 1 was to convert as soon as possible to the aircraft from its existing Fw 190s, also with an establishment of 52 He 162s. Finally, III. *Gruppe* was to replace its Bf 109s with 52 Heinkels during April and May.

On 1 April, four He 162s were handed over to 2./JG 1, and by the 7th two more aircraft had been delivered to the unit, but II./JG 1 still had no He 162s at its disposal. Over the course of the next few days the pilots of JG 1 continued, albeit in limited numbers, with their familiarisation process at Parchim and, slowly but surely, more He 162s trickled in from the factories. On the 4th, Hauptmann Künnecke was in the air in 'White 1' shortly after dawn at 0655 hrs for just eight minutes, while Leutnant Berger followed in He 162 'White 2' for eight minutes at 0725 hrs. Unteroffizier Helmut Riehl of 2./JG 1 made two seven-minute training flights in 'White 1' over Parchim in the early afternoon. Riehl had flown Fw 190s with 2. *Staffel* since early 1944. He had been wounded in action, bailed out and survived and had lodged claims against two B-17s.

Some of the Luftwaffe pilots assisted the works pilots in ferrying in completed aircraft, while others undertook assessment and familiarisation flights, occasionally even in small formations. Fahnenjunker-Feldwebel Günther Kirchner gained his first experience of the Heinkel fighter when he made three conversion flights during the fading evening light of the 4th in 'White 3'. Kirchner was a veteran of 5./JG 1, but had been wounded in action on 11 January 1944 when he had claimed two B-17s shot down during a USAAF raid over central

Germany. Following recovery, he spent some time as an instructor with *Jagdgruppe West* in the summer of 1944, before transferring to I./JG 1 in mid-February 1945.

Unteroffizier Alvo von Alvensleben of 1./JG 1 also learned to fly the He 162 at Parchim at this time;

'When the engine was started up, an unusually loud noise came from the turbine. The aircraft, small and light, with a huge engine on its back, made such a din rolling on the runway that one was relieved when the aircraft lifted off. The wheels left the ground at a speed of 220 km/h. Acceleration was good and a normal runway sufficed. In flight, the aircraft was stable and quiet. It responded easily to the controls. In general, training speeds were between 500 and 700 km/h. In the dive, according to factory information, we could reach the speed of sound. As for myself, I was able to reach 1000 km/h once. We did not have the opportunity to try aerobatics with it though. Lacking experience on the type, and having doubts as to the solidity of the undercarriage, I always touched down as gently as possible. After a very short flight it would land, and once again the noise became appalling. I flew the aircraft on ten occasions.'

Gradually, these pilots developed an understanding of the He 162, its capabilities, limitations and peculiarities. However, this was done against rapidly worsening conditions. On 6 April the USAAF's Eighth Air Force sent 1261 heavy bombers to attack jet airfields and marshalling yards across northern and central Germany, including the airfield at Parchim. The latter was left heavily cratered and the runway rendered unusable. That night all effort was made to conduct repairs ready for a transfer to Ludwigslust at the soonest moment in order to continue with the training process.

The next day, official orders came through from OKL instructing the *Stab*/JG 1 to transfer from Garz to Ludwigslust, where it was to join I. *Gruppe*, and for II./JG 1 to relocate from Garz to Warnemünde. This *Gruppe* was under the command of Hauptmann Paul-Heinrich Dähne, a native of Frankfurt/Oder. Dähne, known by his nickname of 'Sarotti', had accumulated almost 100 victories, achieved whilst serving with 2./JG 52 in Russia and then 12./JG 11 in the *Reichsverteidigung*. He had been awarded the Ritterkreuz on 6 April 1944 in recognition of his 74th victory, and by the time of his death would be accredited with at least 98 victories scored over an operational career that involved some 600 missions.

II./JG 1 had already begun preparing for its move to Warnemünde, from where it would embark on its conversion to the He 162 at nearby Rostock-Marienehe. On 5 April 8./JG 1 had been disbanded and its pilots and Fw 190A-8s assigned to a *Schlachtgeschwader*. The *Staffelkapitän* of 8./JG 1, Hauptmann Wolfgang Ludewig, was reassigned to take command of 7./JG 1, whose *Kapitän*, Leutnant Günther Heckmann, had transferred to 10./JG 7 in March. However, 5./JG 1 had been without a leader since the death of its *Kapitän*, Leutnant Hubert Swoboda, on 11 March, while similarly 6./JG 1 had been without a commander since Oberleutnant Fritz Wegener had transferred to JG 7 the previous month to fly the Me 262.

One pilot who was fortunate enough to miss the attack on Parchim was Leutnant Rudolf Schmitt of 1./JG 1. He had gone to EHAG at Rostock-Marienehe, from where he ferried He 162 Wk-Nr 120068 to Ludwigslust that afternoon. By this time, Schmitt had flown the *Volksjäger*

Hauptmann Paul-Heinrich Dähne, the *Gruppenkommandeur* of II./JG 1. A former member of 2./JG 52 and 12./JG 11, and awarded the Knight's Cross on 6 April 1944, he would eventually be credited with 98 victories, although his final tally is believed to be higher than that figure. He was known to 'distrust' the He 162 and would meet his death in the aircraft on 24 April 1945

Pilots of 3./JG 1 stand close to a bombed-out hangar at Parchim airfield in late March 1945 during the *Staffel's* working-up period on the He 162. Centre, looking at the camera, is the *Staffelkapitän*, Oberleutnant Karl-Emil Demuth, while to his left is Feldwebel Rolf Ackermann

on a number of occasions. Known by the moniker 'Toni-Toni' on account of the two 'ts' in his name, he had joined the Luftwaffe at 18 years of age as a Fahnenjunker and been sent to *Luftkriegschule* 2 at Berlin-Gatow in August 1943. He was moved to *Flugzeugführerschule* C 6 at Kolberg, where he remained until May 1944 when he transferred to 2./JG 107 in Hungary until September. Then followed a spell with 5. and 6./JG 108 at Wiener-Neustadt until 16 February 1945, when Schmitt was posted to 1./JG 1.

Leutnant Gerhard Stiemer of 3. *Staffel*, who had been credited with the destruction of a B-17 and a P-51 while flying the Fw 190, also went to collect an He 162 from Rostock on 8 April, along with Leutnant Köttgen. Stiemer recalled;

'Before takeoff we learned that Parchim had been badly attacked, and due to damage on the runway it would not be possible to land there. We had received enough fuel for only 30 minutes of flying, and flew in the afternoon to Ludwigslust. Over Parchim we saw the destruction on the airfield and the runway. We returned to Parchim during the evening in a lorry.'

The next day would not be a good one for Stiemer;

'During the night, the runway was repaired. The unit could now transfer to Ludwigslust [which had no runway, as it was only a grass field]. During the afternoon I flew with a 162 to Ludwigslust. Because of a defect in the hydraulics for the flaps, the runway wasn't long enough, so I ended up "standing on my head" in a ditch on the airfield perimeter.'

Meanwhile, the pilots of II./JG 1 arrived at Warnemünde by train. They included Unteroffiziere Brück, Emmel, Konrad Augner, Willo Widmann and Wilhelm Harder, Feldwebel Willi Gehrlein, Josef Gold, Erwin Steeb, 'Sepp' Kreutz and Christlieb Fenger and Oberfähnrich Feldt. On 11 April several of these pilots arrived at Rostock-Marienehe, where Carl Francke and other EHAG technical personnel, designers and engineers welcomed them in a brief ceremony.

At this point I./JG 1 had 13-16 He 162s on strength, of which 10-12 were flight-ready for the 40 pilots on hand that were about to commence their conversion training. The *Gruppe* was making at most ten flights per day. II./JG 1 was still waiting for its own He 162s and had only 19 pilots to hand. Unteroffizier Konrad Augner of 8./JG 1 recalled II. *Gruppe's* initial experiences with the He 162 at EHAG Rostock;

'The officers were lodged in a hotel at Warnemünde, with the remaining pilots on the airfield. Each morning, as workers headed for work, a bus or wagon collected us and took us to Marienehe airfield. It was an unusual place, with three runways set out in a triangle in the middle of marshland. First of all, we received theoretical training on the aircraft we would be flying. Then we learned to start the engine, increase the throttle progressively and move onto the runway. We sat in this aircraft as if in a glider.

'Starting the engine was a completely different procedure to that of the Bf 109. The revs had to be increased slowly, while holding the aircraft still with the help of the brakes, up to the moment when one decided that there was sufficient power for takeoff. Releasing the brakes, takeoff was achieved at around 180 km/h. After retracting the undercarriage, we also retracted the flaps. We climbed at around 450-500 km/h.

'This aircraft had a mortal fault. At less than 300 km/h you had to be on your guard against tight turns. If such a turn was attempted the ailerons constrained the circulation of air around the turbine, causing the He 162 to skid and fall like a leaf without any possibility of correcting it. Generally, we only flew for about 35 minutes at fairly low level. However, we also made several flights at 8000 m. We would then be in the air for over an hour. The manoeuvrability of the aircraft was good. For landing, we approached the runway at about 250-260 km/h, and touched down at 200 km/h. It was a totally new flying sensation.'

He 162 'White 21' undergoes maintenance at Ludwigslust. The pilot of the aircraft is visible in the cockpit and a generator cart is in position. Jet efflux appears to be clouding the rear of the BMW 003 engine, indicating a possibly imminent takeoff

To the south in Vienna conditions had become dire. During the course of a visit there, the RLM's *Fliegerstabsing*, Paul Bader, sent the following report to his superiors at Rechlin;

'Commencement of testing is made difficult without spare parts. Organisation in Vienna area has been lost. Performance-measuring, power unit testing and air firing continue. Still no results. Power unit difficulties arise when starting and during flight owing to condition of the jets. Of 12 aircraft, ten have been delivered with a leak-proof wing tank. The weather as yet has no effect on parts constructed of wood. R/T receivers are lacking. Air safety is endangered owing to enemy situation. Support is requested by means of deliveries from Rostock. Number of takeoffs – 25. Flying time – 7 hours 40 minutes. Pilots who have completed conversion – 9.'

On 13 April those He 162s that remained at Parchim were moved to Ludwigslust. Here, training continued, but it was a process that still presented dangerous challenges even to the more experienced pilots. Indeed, Wolfgang Wollenweber believed that several of the senior officers assigned to the He 162 still harboured a 'deep dislike' for the aircraft. On the 12th, Leutnant Karl-Emil Demuth was endeavouring to instruct an over-confident young Fähnrich on the He 162 at Ludwigslust. The latter was the son of a senior Luftwaffe medical officer, and he had apparently been taught to fly by no less a figure than the famed aviatrix Hannah Reitsch.

In his memoirs, Wollenweber indicates that Demuth felt uncomfortable in teaching the youngster, so Wollenweber took over the job. He attempted to ensure that the impatient Fähnrich had really absorbed his instructions before he took off on his first flight in the *Volksjäger*. The Fähnrich assured Wollenweber that he had, but the former *Zerstörer* pilot doubted him. Nevertheless, the aircraft was made ready, and the trainee began his takeoff run. As Wollenweber recalled, 'He wasn't picking up speed quickly enough. Demuth and I could both see what was coming. We both jumped into the Kübelwagen and raced off down the runway'.

As the He 162 made its way 'slowly' down the runway, so it failed to lift off the ground in time and ploughed into a low earth embankment on the edge of the airfield. The Heinkel turned over and skidded along on its engine unit, its right wing breaking away in the process and jet fuel drenching the pilot, who was left upside down in the cockpit. The pilot was fortunate enough to have been able to release himself from the aircraft without the outbreak of a fire, emerging 'sodden and stinking to high heaven of aviation fuel', Wollenweber recorded. 'He stood in front of us wordlessly, holding up his broken index finger!' The stench was too much for Demuth, who made the hapless youngster walk his way back along the runway to dispersal. That afternoon Wollenweber was in the air again, this time in He 162 Wk-Nr 120078, on a 20-minute test flight over Ludwigslust.

Tragedy struck I. *Gruppe* on the 14th when one of its most experienced pilots, Feldwebel Friedrich Enderle of 3. *Staffel*, who had a personal tally of three B-17s shot down, crashed moments after takeoff from Ludwigslust. It was observed that the aircraft failed to climb and exploded on the airfield boundary. An automatic retraction of the flaps was suspected.

Rudi Schmitt flew 'White 7' from Ludwigslust to Husum at 1540 hrs on the 15th and came into contact with a Spitfire south of Hamburg, but, as per orders, he did not attempt to engage. That day, with the military situation facing German forces on the Western Front almost hopeless and with the Allied armies drawing ever nearer, I./JG 1 began its journey north by land and in the air, under the command of Oberleutnant Demuth. It was attempting to escape the British 21st Army Group for as long as it could, relocating from Ludwigslust to Leck, close to the Danish border, from where it was envisaged combat operations with the He 162 would commence.

Even this would prove to be a dangerous task for some pilots. Gerhard Stiemer's aircraft had been fitted with a 1300-litre tank, but burdened by the additional fuel, it needed more distance than usual to take off. When Stiemer eventually got his wheels off the ground, his left wing hit a radio mast to the side of the runway. Using all his strength, Stiemer managed to turn the Heinkel back towards the airfield and land without any further damage.

One by one, JG 1's He 162s made their way north. Wolfgang Wollenweber, flying Wk-Nr 120074, left Ludwigslust at 1755 hrs and touched down in Husum at 1835 hrs. He would continue to Leck on the 16th in 'White 22'. Gerhard Hanf took 'White 1', leaving Ludwigslust at 1500 hrs and arriving at Husum 40 minutes later. Hans Berger managed to fly directly to Leck, arriving there in 'Yellow 5' at 1750 hrs. Adalbert Schlarb left Ludwigslust at 1650 hrs flying He 162 '7', and he staged via Husum but did not move on to Leck until the following day, reaching his destination in the same aircraft at 1645 hrs on the 16th. Schlarb may have experienced technical problems. Günther Kirchner conducted a '*Wetterflug*' (meteorological flight) from Leck

Feldwebel Friedrich Enderle of 3./JG 1 peers at the camera from the open cockpit of an He 162. Enderle had flown missions in the defence of the Reich, during which he had accounted for three B-17s shot down. He was killed when his He 162 crashed at Ludwigslust on 14 April 1945

that day at 1150 hrs in 'Yellow 2', returning at 1216 hrs. This may have been a general reconnaissance for the rest of the *Gruppe*. Gerhard Stiemer made a second attempt to head for Leck following his mishap during takeoff the day before, this time accompanied by Unteroffizier Josef Rieder. The pair of Heinkels was subjected to AA fire over Hamburg, however, and were forced to put down at Husum.

Heinz Künnecke did not leave Ludwigslust until the 17th, reaching Husum in 'White 4' at 1835 hrs. He landed at Leck the next day in the same machine some time after 1600 hrs. Also on the 17th, Stiemer and Rieder attempted to reach Leck once again. For Stiemer it would be his third attempt, and he took off and had a problem-free flight, but Rieder failed to lift off the runway sufficiently due to a fault with his flaps and he crash-landed, suffering injuries to his spine. At the same time, Wolfgang Wollenweber had just landed at Ludwigslust in Wk-Nr 120074 'Red 22', and had spotted the wreckage of Rieder's aircraft. He recalled;

'I brought "Red 22" to a stop, jumped out of the cockpit and started running towards the scene of the crash. [Rieder] was still in the cockpit, unconscious and with blood streaming down his face. Luckily, the canopy had been torn off as well, so I was able to unstrap him and, with the help of some others, lift him out of his seat.'

Rieder was placed in an ambulance and taken to hospital in Leck.

The next day, Unteroffizier Wolfgang Hartung of 2./JG 1 was killed in a crash during his transfer to Leck. Helmut Riehl flew in He 162 'White 5' from Ludwigslust to Husum in the mid-afternoon, then made the short hop from Husum to Leck, landing at 1830 hrs after a 15-minute flight. He had passed close to six Spitfires en route, but there was no engagement.

By 19 April the He 162 had finally been deployed operationally. I./JG 1 was assigned to patrol the airspace over Schleswig-Holstein and to defend against RAF fighters and fighter-bombers that were operating, almost at will, against German troop movements and conducting general low-level interdiction missions in the area. However, the meagre numbers of operationally ready aircraft thwarted the *Gruppe's* ability to carry out its mission in anything more than *Rotte* strength.

At 1222 hrs on the 19th, a *Rotte* from 3./JG 1, comprising Leutnant Stiemer and Fahnenjunker-Feldwebel Günther Kirchner, was scrambled from Leck to intercept enemy fighters reported to be in the vicinity. Stiemer led, with Kirchner following about 30 metres behind and to the right as the two Heinkels took off. But when less than 50 m from the ground, two 'P-47 Thunderbolts' suddenly flashed across their line of sight from behind. Stiemer glanced over his shoulder just in time to see the canopy of Kirchner's aircraft blow away and the pilot's ejection seat shoot into the air. However, due to the low altitude, Kirchner's parachute failed to open and the pilot 'fell to his death'.

A less commonly seen rear view of the He 162 showing the exhaust of the BMW 003 jet engine and the open undercarriage doors. The photograph was probably taken at Leck in May 1945 but after the cessation of hostilities, since the men gathered by the tent are British. Three Bf 109s are visible in the background

Leutnant Gerhard Stiemer of 3./JG 1. Although an experienced fighter pilot, he, like several other Luftwaffe airmen, found the He 162 difficult to master and experienced mishaps on more than one occasion, culminating in a particularly bad crash-landing on 25 April 1945 when he was knocked unconscious and suffered injuries to both of his legs

It is doubtful that the enemy aircraft Stiemer saw were P-47s, for the only American fighters that could possibly have been in the area that day were P-51s. Officially, the Eighth Air Force did not fly Thunderbolts to Germany that day and the Ninth Air Force was operating much further south. Of the 546 P-51s despatched by the Eighth Air Force that day, two were lost. Instead, Wolfgang Wollenweber recounts that, in fact, they were aircraft belonging to the RAF's 2nd Tactical Air Force, whose Hawker Tempest Vs were engaged in wide-ranging fighter sweeps against German airfields that day. It is entirely possible that Stiemer mistook Tempests for P-47s.

According to Wollenweber, Kirchner, using his rudder, put his aircraft into a sharp, 180-degree turn. 'This was something the He 162 simply would not stand for', remembered Wollenweber. The aircraft rolled over onto its back and fell to the ground 'like an autumn leaf'. At that moment, Wollenweber witnessed Kirchner make 'his second, and final mistake of the day' by firing the ejection seat, which, rather than pushing him upwards, shot him at the ground. This was, however, the first known incident of a pilot deploying the catapult seat installed in the He 162. Kirchner's abandoned aircraft, 'Yellow 2', crashed near the village of Klintum, 4 km south of Leck. Stiemer, meanwhile, turned around but was unable to lower his undercarriage. He managed to land safely nevertheless.

Meanwhile, the Tempest V pilot had opened fire on the stricken Heinkel, but was then fired at by the Leck flak battery. The pilot was forced to crash-land close to the nearby village of Niebüll and was taken to the local police station, where an angry mob had gathered baying for his blood. The RAF airman was saved by timely intervention on the part of Wollenweber, who drove him in a *Kübelwagen* back to Leck. From here he was eventually taken off to a PoW camp.

Among the 2nd TAF units attacking German airfields that morning was a formation of eight Tempest Vs from No 135 Wing's No 222 (Natal) Sqn. The unit strafed the airfields at Schlisburg and Husum, claiming one enemy aircraft destroyed and eight damaged. The Tempest Vs were over the latter target at 1220 hrs and at 1000 ft when one of the pilots, Flg Off Geoffrey Walkington, spotted an aircraft flying away from the airfield at 500 ft. In his subsequent combat report Walkington recorded;

'I was flying as "Blue 1" strafing Husum airfield when I sighted an aircraft flying in a northerly direction away from the aerodrome. I immediately broke off my attack on the airfield and chased this aircraft, which was camouflaged mottled green with a yellow underside and appeared to have twin fins and rudders and one engine. The nose of the aircraft had a drooping appearance and the wings (plan view) resembled those of an Me 109. Due to my loss of speed on turning, the enemy aircraft pulled away to about 1500 yards.

'Having recognised this aircraft as hostile by its camouflage, I gave chase, but was unable to close, my IAS [indicated airspeed] being 360 mph. The enemy aircraft did a 360-degree turn to starboard, which I followed, turning inside. During my turn I managed to close to 1000 yards. Being unable to gain further I trimmed my aircraft carefully and, allowing about three-quarters of a ring above the enemy aircraft, I fired short bursts. The enemy aircraft then pulled up through cloud, which was eight-tenths at 3000 ft. I followed through a gap and passed the enemy aircraft spinning down out of control from approximately 3500 ft. I then watched the enemy aircraft explode on the ground near Husum aerodrome.'

Walkington claimed 'one unidentified enemy aircraft destroyed', having expended 150 rounds of semi-armour-piercing ammunition and 150 rounds of high-explosive ammunition, but whether his victim was an He 162 is not clear. Certainly his description of the aircraft having 'twin fins and rudders and one engine' suggests an He 162 and, as has been mentioned, Heinkels of I./JG 1 were flying in and out of Husum by this time. As far as is known, however, only one He 162 has been recorded as lost that day – the aircraft of Fahnenjunker-Feldwebel Kirchner at Leck at roughly the same time, but 35.1 km to the north. It is possible that Walkington shot down another type of aircraft. Whatever the case, the day's events remain a mystery, but the Luftwaffe nevertheless had suffered its first He 162 operational loss on the first day the aircraft went into action.

Meanwhile, flight training continued on the 19th, both at I./JG 1's new Leck base and at Rostock-Marienehe – Oberleutnant Wollenweber performed a training flight over the former location in He 162 'Yellow 11', while at Marienehe, Unteroffizier Herbert Dosch, who had joined 5./JG 1 from J.Gr West, flew the He 162 twice that morning (his first flights in the Heinkel). Likewise, Feldwebel Erwin 'Sepp' Steeb, who had been with II./JG 1 since December 1943, made his introductory flight in an He 162 numbered '5' that same day.

By 20 April the Soviet Army was only some 16 km from the northeastern outskirts of Berlin and the city shook with the impact of continuous Russian shelling. OKL signalled various commands that I. and II./JG 1 together with III./JG 301 were to be placed under the control of *Luftflottenkommando Reich* and were to operate in the 'north area' with the He 162 and Ta 152, respectively. The men of I./JG 1 continued some form of training and testing as word came through that II./JG 1 could expect delivery of ten He 162s by the end of April.

Leutnant Schlarb took off from Leck at 1012 hrs on the 20th and embarked on an 8400 m high-altitude flight in He 162 '7'. At some point during the day JG 1 launched four aircraft to engage RAF Typhoons reported to be in the Leck area attacking ground targets. The pilots had spent their time, as usual, sitting on the grass by the edge of the airfield close to the Heinkels, which had the starter carts connected. When the 'Start' order came through, He 162s Yellow '1', '3', '7' and '11' were prepared for operation, but 'Yellow 1' and Oberleutnant Wollenweber's 'Yellow 3' both had problems starting up. After three unsuccessful attempts to start '3', Wollenweber told the other three pilots to go ahead without him. He then waited another ten minutes, tried a fourth time and the turbine spun into life. He took off immediately.

Over the radio, Wollenweber heard that the other three pilots had failed to locate the enemy and, due to the limits of endurance, had turned back. He climbed to 3000 m and made course for Husum. Wollenweber released the safety switch to his cannon, but then discovered that his Revi 16 gunsight was malfunctioning. He duly resorted to the fold-out manual sight, which was working;

'In front of me I saw Husum airfield, from which I could see smoke rising from the ground defences. I pushed on, and at 900 km/h I came straight

Flg Off Geoffrey Walkington of No 222 (Natal) Sqn (right), who claimed 'one unidentified enemy aircraft destroyed' that he described as having 'twin fins and rudders and one engine' over Husum on 19 April 1945. It is possible that his victim was Fahnenjunker-Feldwebel Kirchner of 3./JG 1

Feldwebel Erwin Steeb, seen in the cockpit of an Fw 190, joined II./JG 1 in December 1943. Transferring to 1./JG 1, he flew the He 162 for the first time on 19 April 1945. It is probable that Steeb was flying Wk-Nr 310005 'Yellow 5' when he was forced to bail out two days later

He 162 Wk-Nr 120072 'Yellow 3' at Leck in May 1945. The aircraft was flown variously by Oberleutnant Wolfgang Wollenweber and Leutnant Gerhard Stiemer of 2. and 3./JG 1, respectively, but it carries the emblem of 3./JG 1, depicting the Lion of Danzig. The item resting on the nose is not a parachute, but rather Oberleutnant Wollenweber's personal briefcase

into the flight path of the attacking British, who were concentrating on the ground targets. I took the last aircraft in my sight and at a range of around 100 m pushed the firing button, but it was "silence in the woods". The weapons did nothing. I flew to the next Typhoon and overflew his cockpit canopy by just five metres and then pushed the throttle through to full power and flew into the heavens, and that was a bit of a shock and a surprise for the British. They immediately broke off their ground-attack and tried to follow me, which was like someone on a moped trying to catch a Porsche.'

In frustration, Wollenweber thumped the Revi sight but to no avail. At that point, however, the British fighters broke off their strafing attacks and headed back over the coast for their base. It was now time for Wollenweber to return home too;

'I then had the problem of trying to find Leck, where there would be waiting fighters. I was not reassured by the report that there was a low-level attack in progress on the airfield. I then solved the problem by making a low-level flight from Niebüll along the road to Leck at 300 km/h, and landed on the concrete runway where the last bits of rubber had been stripped away. Nevertheless, I managed to get back in one piece.'

On landing, Wollenweber erroneously described in his logbook that the fighters he had intercepted were 'Thunderbolts'. Shortly thereafter, another scramble order was given and Leutnant Berger took off in Leutnant Stiemer's usual aircraft – He 162 'Red 1' – but he landed back at Leck apparently without incident.

That afternoon Leutnant Hanf scrambled in He 162A-2 Wk-Nr 120077 'Red 1', which carried a distinctive personal emblem with the inscription *Nervenklau* (Nerve Jangler). 'The unusual white "*Nervenklau*" marking suddenly appeared one day on the left-hand fuselage of my He 162', recounted Hanf. 'This was the creation of our technicians, whose rest in their quarters I regularly disturbed with my motorcycle, which was always honking. I didn't want to be a killjoy, so I accepted the emblem with a smile'. Hanf flew a second patrol that afternoon, but neither was eventful.

For others, however, it was to be a less fortunate day resulting in the loss of two precious aircraft. Leutnant Schmitt bailed out, apparently using his ejection seat, near Leck following a technical problem with his aircraft during a familiarisation flight, while Unteroffizier Gerhard Fendler of 2./JG 1 was killed when his Heinkel crashed while on a ferry flight.

On the afternoon of 21 April 'Sepp' Steeb took off on his third training flight of the day in He 162 '5', but he was forced to bail out when the aircraft malfunctioned near Dierkow. Whether he actually ejected is not known. The next day, there were more scrambles. Firstly, Hauptmann Künnecke took off leading a small formation from Leck in He 162 'White 7'

at 0955 hrs, followed a minute later by his wingman, Unteroffizier Riehl, in 'White 4', and, a minute after him, Leutnant Hanf, in 'Red 1'. It seems the patrol was without event, however, and that afternoon Hanf was on another patrol in 'Red 1' accompanied by Leutnant Hans Berger in 'White 4', who took off five minutes later. Both pilots returned safely. Hanf was despatched on two *Alarmstarts* in He 162 'Red 1' from Leck the next morning, although both flights were ultimately without incident.

Even at this late stage in the war new He 162s were being delivered from Rostock to both Warnemünde and Leck, but on occasion with catastrophic results. Feldwebel Rolf Ackermann of 3./JG 1 was killed in a crash on landing at Leck from a ferry flight during the afternoon of the 23rd. There was growing evidence that either pilots were still not adequately trained to fly the jet or that the He 162 was proving a difficult machine to master – or both. The latter was confirmed the next afternoon at Warnemünde when Hauptmann Paul-Heinrich Dähne, the *Gruppenkommandeur* of II./JG 1 and a holder of the Knight's Cross, was killed.

At a height of less than 500 m, Dähne commenced a turn that quickly resulted in the He 162 'skidding' through the air. It then somersaulted out of control, with white smoke streaming from its BMW 003 engine. The jet began to rapidly lose height, Konrad Augner of 8./JG 1 witnessing the scene from the airfield. He remembered;

'It fell like a dead leaf and crashed in the marsh at the mouth of the Warne. The *Gruppenkommandeur* had probably tried to bail out without first having jettisoned the canopy, and had smashed his skull. That would explain the splinters of glass. We immediately jumped into boats to go to his aid. We searched in vain.'

Augner's theory is given credence by the recollection of Unteroffizier Wilhelm Harder;

'The He 162 had a very evil habit. When you accelerated to the side, the jet exhaust from the engine forced the rudder to "stick", which meant you couldn't control the machine. It then made a downward movement like a falling leaf from a tree. Once the He 162 went into this movement, there was only one thing to do – jettison the hood, pull up your feet and get out with the catapult seat. This was how our *Gruppenkommandeur* Hauptmann Dähne crashed to his death on his first flight.'

According to Wolfgang Wollenweber, 'Dähne had been one of those pilots who had distrusted and rejected the He 162 from the very outset. He had therefore never tried to come to terms with its strengths and its weaknesses. I suspect he didn't even know of the dangers posed by the misuse of the rudder'. Dähne's successor as *Kommandeur* was Major Werner Zober, a former bomber pilot, a veteran of the Legion Condor and a holder of the Spanienkreuz mit Brillanten (Spanish Cross with Diamonds). Zober had suffered serious wounds during combat and had had a leg amputated. He later served with the *Erprobungsstelle* Rechlin and was then appointed as the first commander of the *E-Stelle* at Udetfeld. Zober had joined JG 1

The He 162A-2 Wk-Nr 120077 'Red 1' of Leutnant Gerhard Hanf of 2./JG 1 at Leck in late April 1945. It bore the name *'Nervenklau'* on the port side as a humorous reference to the pilot's motorcycle, and was also adorned with the wolf's head emblem of III./JG 77, with whom Hanf flew before joining JG 1. Finally, the aircraft also carries the red arrows of JG 1. Note the capped barrel of the MG 151/20 20 mm cannon and the blast staining at the end of the barrel trough, the communication panel in the canopy hood and the Revi 16 B gunsight on top of the instrument panel, visible through the windscreen. The intake of the BMW 003 has been protected by a tarpaulin

He 162A-2 Wk-Nr 120095 'White 20' of JG 1 at Leck in May 1945 after the cessation of hostilities. The aircraft carries the *Geschwader's* red arrow symbols on its nose section, together with what appears to be a two-coloured ring. The intake ring panel of the BMW 003 is also red. The Heinkel next to 'White 20' could be Wk-Nr 120231

Unteroffizier Wilhelm Harder of 2./JG 1 first flew the *Volksjäger* on 24 April 1945, and he subsequently recalled that taking off from Rostock-Marienehe was a challenging experience

a few days prior to Dähne's death, but it is unlikely that he ever flew the He 162 while with JG 1.

Unteroffizier Wilhelm Harder, who had joined II./JG 1 from 15./EJG 1 in late December 1944, made his first flight in an He 162 from EHAG at Rostock-Marienehe on the 24th;

'The single intact runway was barely 1000 m long and it was bordered to the east by the Breitling [a stretch of water at the mouth of the Warnow] and to the west by the Rostock-Warnemünde railway line. Of course the takeoff distance for such a bird was a really tough one, especially due to the railway line, with its obligatory telegraph cables.

'The He 162 was also so placed that the takeoff was very close to the Breitling – Herr Francke took steps to sort that out. Initial acceleration was very sluggish. The thing rolled along the runway like a lit-up toy mouse and used up almost the length of the runway. At the end, you literally had to pull up sharp so as to avoid the telegraph cables, and there it would hang in the air like a ripe plumb. [Francke] landed so coolly as if it was a Klemm 35 [trainer] and not a jet fighter, but in doing so he used the whole of the runway to the last metre.

'Over the next few days there was further instruction in technical aspects, servicing and, eventually, flight control on a practical basis in the machine, and finally the engine was started. All this practising took up a lot of time and, eventually, after every run-up, the engine had to be left to cool down. During this period we were constantly given further instruction and advice. Now and again, the "blowtorch" didn't light up, and if it didn't start, we had to clean all the pipes out before we could start up again. Then the tail would have to be pushed down so that the fuel "brew" would drain out and the rest of the interior workings had to be cleaned out with a rag and washed down, and then the bird would be ready for another takeoff.

'Around 20 April 1945 training was put into practice. We each had to make a flight of about 20 minutes in the He 162. I say "around", because I believe I made my first flight on 24 April 1945 – and because I was then an Unteroffizier I was well back in the ranks.'

Joining JG 1 in February 1945 from an Me 262 training course at Lechfeld was Major Bernd Gallowitsch. An Austrian born in Vienna in February 1918, Gallowitsch entered an Austrian pilot school in 1936, but in 1939 he transferred to the Luftwaffe to serve as a bomber pilot in KG 100, with whom he flew pathfinder missions. He converted to fighters and joined IV./JG 51 in June 1940 fighting with the unit over the English Channel and scoring his first victory. Gallowitsch then served on the Russian Front with 12./JG 51 until he was badly wounded. When he left the front, he had accounted for 64 enemy aircraft shot down and 23 tanks destroyed in 840 combat missions, during the course of which he was shot down five times himself.

Gallowitsch was awarded the Ritterkreuz on 24 January 1942 on the occasion of his 42nd victory, and later that year he was transferred to the Staff of the OKL, before being assigned to Lechfeld for jet training. Later, when with JG 1, he took part in the move by road at night from Ludwigslust to Husum. Gallowitsch suffered slight injuries, along with Oberleutnant Wilhelm Krebs, the Technical Officer of I./JG 1, when the car in which he was travelling collided with another vehicle on a darkened road, both cars moving without the benefit of lights.

From late April to the end of the war, the 'I. *Einsatzgruppe*/JG 1' was given 'freedom of operations' by OKL to operate in the ground-attack role. However, only a few such operations were flown in an attempt to strafe enemy columns on the roads between Leck and Husum, Heide and Schleswig and Flensburg and Leck. On one such mission on the 25th, Leutnant Schmitt of 1./JG 1, airborne from Leck at 1120 hrs in 'White 5' on a *Rotteneinsatz* apparently to conduct a ground-attack patrol, was ordered to engage low-flying British Mosquitoes reported to be near Flensburg, but ultimately there was no encounter with the enemy.

That afternoon, on the last occasion they would fly the He 162, Leutnant Berger took off from Leck in 'Yellow 3' on an *Alarmstart* with Leutnant Stiemer. Their mission was to engage 'P-47s' but it was to be without event. Certainly Berger flew his aircraft to the limit of its endurance, and when he landed after 43 minutes, his tanks must have been near empty. However, as Stiemer returned to Leck his fuel was also dangerously low and he crash-landed, being knocked unconscious in the process. Oberleutnant Demuth hurried across the airfield to Stiemer's smouldering aircraft and smashed in the canopy with an axe. Stiemer had suffered injuries to his legs, but given oxygen, he was removed from the cockpit and taken to the hospital in Leck, where he would join Josef Rieder and remain to the end of the war.

On the 26th, Unteroffizier Helmut Rechenbach of 2./JG 1 is alleged to have shot down an enemy aircraft in the *Volksjäger*, making it the type's first combat victory, but certainly the 2nd TAF reported no corresponding losses for this day.

On the 28th, a formation of between eight and twelve He 162s from II./JG 1 transferred to Leck via Kaltenkirchen, but those pilots without aircraft had to make the move by road. Two days later, elements of the *Gruppe* that were reported to be in Mecklenburg on their journey by road

Mechanics prepare He 162 Wk-Nr 310005 'Yellow 5' for flight at Ludwigslust in early April 1945. The canopy is up and the engine tarpaulin removed, suggesting its pilot, possibly Leutnant Hans Berger of 3./JG 1, will shortly enter the cockpit

to Leck were warned that they would have to move to their destination 'under enemy pressure'.

Five days earlier, on the 23rd, Oberleutnant Demuth ordered Oberleutnant Wollenweber to head to EHAG at Rostock-Marienehe along with ten pilots to collect the last He 162s. Wollenweber, whose group included Leutnante Stiemer and Schlarb, set off in a worn-out, wood-burning, Hanomag lorry with the headlights switched off to avoid detection by Allied nightfighters. Reaching Marienehe on the Hanomag's last gasp, Wollenweber immediately asked how many He 162s would be ready to ferry to Leck. 'I was informed that there were just two waiting for us, and that the factory would be producing only one machine a day from now on', Wollenweber recalled. Despatching Stiemer and another pilot to take the two available machines, he 'had a nose around the works to see if there were any other aircraft we might "borrow" if the need arose. Russian tanks were getting ever closer'.

In the air, attrition escalated for II./JG 1. On 30 April Leutnant Hans Rechenberg of that *Gruppe* was shot at by a Spitfire while ferrying an He 162 from Rostock to Leck. Rechenberg's aircraft crashed near Wismar, but he escaped the wreckage unhurt. Erwin Steeb crash-landed near Kaltenkirchen and Oberfeldwebel Karl Beck, also of II./JG 1, crashed near Klintum as a result of fuel exhaustion while flying to Leck. Leutnant Schlarb took off in He 162 Wk-Nr 120099 on a ferry flight from Rostock, but crash-landed 15 minutes later east of Kiel probably as a result of fuel shortage caused by a faulty gauge. Finally, Leutnant Dürr took off from Rostock-Marienehe to ferry Wk-Nr 120086 to Leck in the afternoon, but he was forced to land on the Autobahn north of Dänischburg, near Lübeck, also due to a lack of fuel. He would fly the *Volksjäger* for the last time on 2 May.

At Rostock-Marienehe, Oberleutnant Wollenweber, Fähnrich Köhler and Unteroffiziere Helmut Riehl and Anton Riemer were informed by an EHAG engineer that there remained just one, possibly two, aircraft to come off the production line before it was shut down prior to the factory being closed and evacuated. The little good news was that these machines would have additional fuel capacity, allowing them to remain in the air for longer. The problem was locating the fuel, and as the airmen began to search the factory for it, members of the EHAG management were preparing to fly out in Ju 52/3ms and any other aircraft they could find available.

The end was drawing near. Adolf Hitler had committed suicide in Berlin on 30 April, where German troops were street-fighting the Russians. On 1 May British forces under Field Marshal Bernard Montgomery continued their drive across northern Germany and advanced from the Elbe towards the German capital virtually unopposed. Soviet forces had almost reached the Heinkel works at Rostock. At Leck, the *Geschwaderkommodore* of JG 1, Oberstleutnant Ihlefeld, assembled his men and informed them of the *Führer*'s death. He also told them that he no longer had any right to detain them, and that they were free to go if they so wished. He suggested that the *Geschwader* remain together until the airfield was taken by the British, however. It seems his suggestion was met with unanimous agreement.

At Marienehe, the two last *Volksjäger* did eventually arrive from the assembly halls. Wollenweber ordered Riemer (in Wk-Nr 120100) and Riehl (in Wk-Nr 120104) to fly them to Leck. Early on the morning of 1 May they took off, with the Russians just 10 km from the EHAG plant.

Riehl's aircraft suffered mechanical problems and came down just beyond the factory airfield boundary, while Riemer's Heinkel crashed on its way to Leck, the pilot being injured. Wollenweber and Riehl managed to escape Rostock in a Fieseler Storch and made it back to Leck safely.

The *Stab* and II./JG 1 also arrived at Leck with very little equipment. A general reorganisation of JG 1's commanders took place, although it was very fluid. The *Geschwader* is believed to have had approximately 45 He 162s on strength as at 1 May.

On the 2nd, Unteroffizier Herbert Dosch of 5./JG 1 made a 26-minute transfer flight in an unidentified He 162 from Neumünster to Leck. He observed 'six Thunderbolts' on route but did not engage.

By the 3rd, Leck was a crowded airfield, having become a destination for the surviving remnants of several fighter, bomber and nightfighter *Gruppen*. Bf 109s, Fw 190s, Ar 234s, He 162s, He 111s, Ju 88s and He 219s were all marshalled under the composite command of Oberstleutnant Karl-Gottfried Nordmann, the *Inspekteur der Jagdflieger Ost* and *Jafü Nord Ost*. But still JG 1's He 162s flew.

At 1138 hrs on Friday, 4 May, just a few hours before Admiral von Friedeburg, the Chief of Naval Staff, and General Eberhard Kinzel, Chief of the North West Army Command, signed the instrument of surrender of the German forces facing Montgomery's 21st Army Group, Leutnant Rudolf Schmitt took off in He 162 'White 1' from Leck to engage RAF Typhoons. Schmitt subsequently noted in his logbook, '1145 hrs: Typhoon wirksam beschossen' (fired upon with effect) following an encounter southeast of Husum. This term was used customarily by pilots to describe the successful destruction of a ground target. His 'victim' may have been a Typhoon or a Tempest, as both types were operating in the area at the time. Whilst it is unlikely, however, that Schmitt actually shot an aircraft down, he cannot be denied the likelihood that he opened fire 'with effect' on an enemy single-engined fighter or fighter-bomber southeast of Husum and assumed he had damaged the aircraft, perhaps even sufficiently to cause it to go down.

That day, I. and II./JG 1 were ordered to merge as 'I.(*Einsatz*)/JG 1' under Oberstleutnant Ihlefeld, with '1.(*Einsatz*) *Staffel*' under Major Zober and '2.(*Einsatz*) *Staffel*' under Hauptmann Ludewig. However, soon after this, orders arrived from *Luftflottenkommando Mitte* instructing the new *Gruppe* to prepare to hand all its aircraft over to the British and Americans as and when they arrived at Leck. The following morning, 5 May, the *Luftflottenkommando* issued the order to 'cease action'. Some of the Heinkels had had explosives placed in their cockpits ready to be detonated, and they were duly removed.

At Leck, in what must have been one of the final operational flights made by the He 162, Fähnrich Oskar Köhler of 3./JG 1 crashed. Köhler was an experienced flying instructor who had joined the *Geschwader* from JG 105, where he had flown the Fw 190. However, even for someone with Köhler's experience, the hurried transition from piston-engined aircraft to the He 162 could be challenging. Köhler's jet landed on the runway at full speed and slewed to a stop on the airfield boundary. He suffered injuries to his legs and was removed from the wreckage of his aircraft by Oberleutnant Demuth and the *Geschwader* medical officer.

Hours later, British tanks rumbled onto Leck airfield.

CHAPTER FIVE

'THIS JET FIGHTER SHOULD BE STUDIED FURTHER'

Shortly after the German surrender in early May 1945, *Jagdgeschwader* 1 organised its He 162s into two neat rows on Leck airfield in anticipation of the arrival of British air intelligence specialists who were eager to learn more about German jet aircraft technology

For the men of *Jagdgeschwader* 1, the atmosphere at Leck during May 1945 became somewhat surreal. An eerie calm fell over the place as the Germans waited to discover what would become of them and their aircraft.

In an early move, and in accordance with a directive from British forces at the cessation of hostilities, Oberstleutnant Ihlefeld arranged to present the He 162s of his unit for surrender to and inspection by Allied air technical intelligence. The aircraft were gathered from their dispersed and scattered locations around the airfield, where they had been left to minimise the effect of strafing by enemy aircraft, and marshalled into two, neat rows of nine and 13 aircraft, with their noses facing each other along one of the taxi tracks. Any explosives had been removed from the Heinkels, with the only 'defiant' measures taken by the Germans being the removal of the Riedel starter motors and the blocking of the rudders. These measures effectively immobilised the *Volksjäger*, but not sufficiently to prevent them being made airworthy again without difficulty.

On 6 May a convoy of light armour and lorries carrying RAF personnel arrived at Leck. Oberst Nordmann, together with Ihlefeld, met the British in

an atmosphere of cautious cordiality. Handshakes were exchanged. The German officers were informed that as long as they cooperated, they would be allowed to retain their sidearms. An agreement was reached between the British and the Germans, and Ihlefeld instructed his staff accordingly. The bulk of the British units departed.

A view of the taxi track at Leck towards the right-hand row of He 162s, showing Wk-Nr 120013 'White 1' also adorned with the emblem of 1./JG 1 and believed to be the aircraft of Leutnant Rudolf Schmitt. Bernburg-built Wk-Nr 310078 'Yellow 5' next to it was reportedly the aircraft of Hauptmann Heinz Künnecke

He 162 Wk-Nr 120067 'White 4' was the first aircraft in the left-hand row at Leck looking northwest. Only a few of the aircraft had their tarpaulins removed and canopies opened

Life then settled into a subdued rhythm under the May sunshine. Card games became routine, letters were written home and there was a peculiar absence of orders, air raid alarms and flying. The personnel of both *Staffeln* were quartered in the surrounding villages, with 2./JG 1 finding accommodation in a school in the village of Stadum, just to the southeast of the airfield on the road to Flensburg.

Around mid-May, Oberst Ihlefeld called Oberleutnant Wollenweber from Stadum to the airfield. In a strange chain of events, Wollenweber had been appointed acting *Staffelkapitän* of 2.(*Einsatz*) *Staffel*/JG 1 in place of Hauptmann Ludewig who had mysteriously disappeared. Wollenweber duly reported to the *Kommodore* to find him in the company of some RAF officers and technicians including Sqn Ldr R M Cracknell, Engineering Officer at the Royal Aircraft Establishment (RAE) at Farnborough. Ihlefeld explained that the British were intrigued by the He 162 and wished to learn about it. Wollenweber was to explain the aircraft's controls and mechanics and to then perform a demonstration flight in Wk-Nr 120028, 'White 3'. 'I went through the operating handbook with the English pilot', Wollenweber recalled. 'He was not only highly interested in what I had to tell him, but also gave me the impression that he understood all the necessary controls and would be perfectly capable of handling them'.

It is probable that the RAF officer Wollenweber describes was Sqn Ldr Cracknell, who later reported;

'A German pilot and engineer were used to give information about the He 162. The pilot stated before takeoff that he would like to demonstrate it to prove that it was satisfactory, which was reassuring about his good faith. He stated that the 1200 m runway at Leck is only just sufficient as the takeoff and landing run is long. He said the undercarriage is strong and that there is no disadvantage in the narrow track (presumably because of

'Under new ownership'. Leutnant Gerhard Stiemer contemplates a sign intended to make it clear who the new operators of Leck airfield were. Stiemer is resting on a walking stick probably as a result of injuries he sustained to his legs when his He 162 crashed at Leck on 25 April 1945

Probably taken from the roof of a car parked opposite, this photograph shows pilots of I./JG 1 awaiting the arrival of British forces at Leck. From the left can be seen Hauptmann Heinz Künnecke, *Staffelkapitän* of 1./JG 1, Oberleutnant Karl-Emil Demuth, the *Staffelführer* of 3./JG 1, Major Werner Zober, who acted as a nominal *Gruppenkommandeur* of I./JG 1 in May 1945, Hauptmann Rahe, *Kommandeur* of II./JG 1, and Hauptmann Wolfgang Ludewig, *Staffelkapitän* of 2./JG 1. The latter two officers are looking at Wk-Nr 120231 'White 6'

the good tricycle characteristics). He stated that there is a variation of up to 100 km/h in the top speed of different aeroplanes. He also said that the undercarriage release might be stiff and that two hands should be used if necessary. He laid great emphasis on the need for flying with the bubble central and using a minimum of rudder. He said that crashes had occurred through a yaw-roll oscillation, which can build up until the aircraft goes out of control if the rudder is used. This is more likely to occur when flaps and undercarriage are down, and he recommended a long, straight approach. He said that this aircraft will not spin.'

However, when Wollenweber went to put on his flying gear the RAF officers stopped him. It seems British trust did not extend as far as allowing a former Luftwaffe pilot to fly off in a jet fighter. The indignant Germans accepted the situation as best they could and watched as the British pilot took off in 'White 3' and made a competent circuit of the airfield. When he landed he remarked to the Luftwaffe officers how impressed he was with the *Volksjäger*.

On 29 May Gp Capt G Mungo Buxton, the Chief Technical Officer at the Central Fighter Establishment (CFE) based at Tangmere, together with Sqn Ldr Cracknell, landed at Schleswig airfield. From here they would journey out to examine and assess captured German aircraft and aeronautical equipment. After conducting an extensive tour of airfields in northern Germany and Denmark, they returned to Schleswig with a list of 42 aircraft to be ferried to the United Kingdom for 'research and trials'. However, this list did not include the He 162 on the basis that its range was 'unknown, but believed to be too small'.

Meanwhile, the Enemy Aircraft Flight of the CFE had established a working party at Leck to attend to any mechanical or technical problems with the He 162s. In a report prepared by Flt Lt R T H Collis, commanding the Flight, it was stated that 'ten He 162s had been made serviceable at Leck and were ready to fly, when a last minute inspection showed the wooden control surfaces to have been affected by weather, and the machines were grounded pending further examination by a British Engineer (Sqn Ldr Cracknell). Two spare turbines and a collection of He 162 parts and tools were assembled at Leck. Ten special parachutes for the ejector seat of the He 162 had been repacked under supervision and assembled for the use of pilots flying the He 162s'.

It would not be until 2 June that Sqn Ldr Cracknell would make two further assessment flights in an He 162 with the aim of taking readings for the RAE from which a rough estimate of the aircraft's ferrying range could be made. After his flights Cracknell made a report of his experience;

'The first takeoff in a crosswind was prolonged (the throttle may have slipped back slightly) and the aircraft had to be pulled off and it began to do this yaw-roll "falling

leaf" oscillation. The undercarriage was retracted, which is a quick action, and at a safe height the flaps were retracted with marked loss of height. The second takeoff and landing on the 1200 m runway were satisfactory, the wind being about 20 mph and dead in line.

'The Perspex is not optically good, which is rather a disadvantage for landing. Oxygen endurance is small, being exhausted about halfway through the first flight, which lasted 30 minutes. It had been turned on perhaps five minutes before takeoff. On the second flight, which lasted 45 minutes, oxygen was not turned on until about 7000 ft had been reached, and lasted until the descent.

'Cockpit controls are ropey. The flap extending pump must be worked vigorously to start it and the flap can only be extended with comfortable pressure when at low speeds. On the second flight, I made a long, straight approach and slowed to 240 km/h to do this. The undercarriage hydraulic kick-out occurred once before retraction was complete. The undercarriage spring release for extension worked with a strong one-hand pull and the nosewheel can be seen extending through the observation window between the pilot's knees.'

Cracknell also noted that it was difficult to taxi in the Heinkel, and that the aircraft should be towed wherever possible, but that in summary, 'The controls and aiming stability are good and will probably be of great interest to a fighter pilot. Undercarriage and brakes are satisfactory. Endurance is small and the oxygen endurance smaller still'.

Eventually, 11 He 162s formerly belonging to JG 1 would be assigned 'AM' (Air Ministry) numbers by the British at Leck. These numbers, to be applied in white paint, were intended to identify an aircraft as being of interest to technical intelligence personnel at their place of surrender, and as a means of differentiating such machines from the bulk that would, eventually, be scrapped. The technical teams were to report on their selections directly to the Air Ministry's Under Secretary of State, Air Intelligence 2(g) and to the Ministry of Aircraft Production.

Shortly after Cracknell's flights there was a change in policy whereby the RAE assumed full responsibility for the recovery of all German aircraft from the CFE and the latter's groundcrews and pilots were to work under RAE orders. By this stage Flt Lt Collis had reported, 'He 162s serviceable at Leck and waiting for disposal. Spares and tools and 400 gallons of J2 fuel assembled and ready for collection'. The *Volksjäger* were to be moved to England by ship.

Far to the south in Austria, there were apparently 12 completed He 162s at the various EHAG facilities at the time of the German surrender, as well as 'a larger number of fuselages and stabilisers ready to be mounted up'. According to Professor Ernst Heinkel and Karl Frydag, 'Up to ten or twelve aeroplanes, the fittings of which were ready for final mounting in the workshop of our sub-contractors in Vienna, were transported firstly to Ainring and then directed to a small factory near Salzburg'.

With his back to the camera, Oberleutnant Wolfgang Wollenweber, the Kapitän (Flying) of 2./JG 1, supervises work on the BMW 003 engine of He 162 Wk-Nr 120028 'White 3' at Leck in readiness for a trial flight by a British pilot, probably Sqn Ldr R M Cracknell of the RAE Farnborough

Evidently Oberleutnant Wollenweber is unperturbed at the notion of smoking a cigarette in close proximity to aviation fuel as a member of the groundcrew awaits his instructions

Oberleutnant Karl-Emil Demuth poses by the tail fin of He 162A-2 Wk-Nr 120074 'Yellow 11', which has been adorned with his 16 victories. The aircraft also carries the emblem of I./JG 1 and a small '20' next to the main tactical number. Note also the dual-coloured protection plate inserted into the engine intake bearing the number '24'

From left, Hauptmann Wolfgang Ludewig, Hauptmann Heinz Künnecke, Oberleutnant Karl-Emil Demuth and Major Werner Zober chat in front of their now-dormant He 162s. Zober was a former member of the Legion Condor, with whom he had flown bombers in the Spanish Civil War, and later worked at the Luftwaffe's test centre at Rechlin. Note the crude bare metal and filler paste finish to He 162 Wk-Nr 120231 'White 6' behind the officers

On 15 May, all the EHAG drawings and documents which had been hidden in a cellar near the Achensee at Jenbach were handed over to the Allied Commission and placed into the hands of Flt Lts Bingham and Lee of the RAF.

In July, Heinkel and Frydag were flown to England, where, for a brief period, they were given accommodation in a boarding house commandeered by the RAF, before being moved to a former children's home in Wimbledon that had 'a garden surrounded by barbed wire'. A few days later the British commenced their interrogations of the renowned aircraft designer and his general manager and technical director. The emphasis was on jet aircraft and technology. Then, on the 17th, the Germans were driven out to the RAE at Farnborough. Heinkel remembered;

'My heart beat faster when I saw eight airworthy He 162s that had been flown to England undamaged. I read the report of an English test pilot, who had achieved 740 km/h with one, and had described the machine from takeoff to landing as the best in the world.'

Heinkel's recollection was not accurate. The first He 162 to arrive at Farnborough was Wk-Nr 120098 (AM 67) on 11 June. This was followed by Wk-Nr 120076 (AM 59) on 15 June, Wk-Nr 120221 (AM 58) on 16 June, Wk-Nr 120072 (AM 61), Wk-Nr 120097 (AM 64), Wk-Nr 120227 (AM 65) and Wk-Nr 120091 (AM 66) on 31 July, Wk-Nr 120074 (AM 60), Wk-Nr 120095 (AM 63) and a machine with no works number recorded on 10 August (AM 68) and Wk-Nr 120086 (AM 62) on 22 August.

On 29 June Wg Cdr R J 'Roly' Falk, Chief Test Pilot at the RAE, flew Wk-Nr 120076 at Farnborough. He flew it again on 5 July, followed by Sqn Ldr A F Martindale on 6 July and Flt Lt Cleaver on 23 July. None of the aircraft's flights had lasted more than 20 minutes, and its total flying time was 1 hour 30 minutes. The Americans joined in the assessment flights on 2 August when Jack Woolams, the renowned Chief Test Pilot at Bell Aircraft Corporation, flew the He 162 for 15 minutes on a transfer flight from the RAE to RAF Brize Norton, in Oxfordshire, where it was placed in storage. Woolams had been the first man to fly a fighter aircraft coast-to-coast, non-stop, over the United States in September 1942. He had also set a new altitude record of 47,600 ft in the summer of 1943.

British testing of the He 162 remained inactive until 7 September when Capt Eric Brown, a test pilot attached to the Aerodynamics Flight of the Experimental Flying Detachment at the RAE, flew Rostock-built He 162 Wk-Nr 120098 (AM 67). Brown, who already had considerable experience in testing German

aircraft, found that caution was needed when handling the throttle in order to avoid overheating, although he felt that the BMW 003 was superior to the Jumo 004, which powered the Me 262, in that respect. Brown put the Heinkel through its paces, pushing its nose down into a powered dive. 'There was no buffeting or vibration', he recorded, 'and a check on the rate of roll at 400 mph revealed the highest that I ever experienced outside the realm of hydraulically-powered ailerons – the stick force demanded to produce those exhilarating gyrations was delightfully light'.

Brown pulled the He 162 into a loop at 563 km/h and then followed with a few stalls before coming into land at 200 km/h, finding like Cracknell did over Leck, that it took some time to pump down the flaps. 'The approach speed had to be held at 125 mph', Brown remembered, 'almost up to the runway threshold, as there was no question of going round again once the throttle had been moved to idling, and there was, therefore, an inevitable tendency to arrive with excessive speed. This called for good braking, and no German aircraft that I had ever flown had brakes

From left to right, Hauptmann Ludewig, Major Zober, Hauptmann Künnecke and Oberleutnant Demuth. According to Wolfgang Wollenweber, Ludewig disappeared shortly after the surrender but was known to be hiding out in a hut not far from Leck airfield, intending to make his way to Brazil

The *Kommodore* of JG 1, Oberstleutnant Herbert Ihlefeld (far left), joins his men on the taxiway at Leck. Walking away from the group is Hauptmann Gerhard Strasen, *Kommandeur* of III./JG 4, which was also based at Leck at the time. Behind Strasen is Knight's Cross-holder Hauptmann Bernd Gallowitsch, who had flown with JG 51 until being wounded in 1942. He is credited with having flown 840 combat missions, during which time he shot down 64 enemy aircraft and destroyed 23 tanks

He 162 Wk-Nr 120098 speeds down the runway after landing at the RAE Farnborough in England following a test flight in the summer of 1945. Designated AM 67 and coded VH513, the aircraft had been built at Rostock and may have been operated by JG 1 as 'White 2'. Capt Eric Brown described this specific machine as a 'delightful little aeroplane'

Hauptmann Heinz Künnecke of 1./JG 1 stands by his Junkers-built He 162 Wk-Nr 310078 'Yellow 5'. The aircraft carries the diving eagle emblem of 1./JG 1 and the red arrow nose marking of the *Geschwader*. The tarpaulin covering the cockpit has the number '11' on it, indicating that it has been taken from another aircraft

An RAF technician inspects He 162 'White 23' at Leck in May 1945. This machine was almost certainly assigned to the *Kommodore* of JG 1, Oberstleutnant Herbert Ihlefeld, although as far as is known, he never flew the *Volksjäger*. The rear fuselage cone has been removed from the aircraft, which has been jacked up, possibly to test the nosewheel. Next to '23' is Wk-Nr 120233, which had suffered a mainwheel collapse at the time

that came up to British standards. By German standards, however, the He 162's brakes were good'. All in all, he viewed the He 162 as a 'delightful little aeroplane'.

In mid-September the British public got their first view of the *Volksjäger* during an exhibition of captured German aircraft held in Hyde Park, in central London, to coincide with a 'Thanksgiving Week'. Curious Londoners were able to inspect Wk-Nr 120086 (AM 62) flown by Leutnant Alfred Dürr of II./JG 1 when he collected it from Rostock-Marienehe to ferry to Leck on 30 April, and in which he had to make a forced-landing on the Autobahn near Lübeck. Another aircraft that 'went public' for several months was Wk-Nr 120095 (AM 63), which toured the cities of the English Midlands.

Then, on 29 October, Flt Lt Foster flew He 162 Wk-Nr 120072 (AM 61) for the second time, during the opening day of the 'German Aircraft Exhibition' held at the RAE, which showcased German wartime aircraft, equipment and weapons. The event drew thousands of visitors from the aviation industry, the armed forces, civil service and, during its closing days in early November, the general public. Also on static display were He 162s Wk-Nr 120097 (AM 64) and Wk-Nr 120091 (AM 66), the latter having been given the RAF serial number VN153. A few days later, however, on 9 November, Flt Lt R A Marks chose to fly a demonstration in Wk-Nr 120072 (AM 61) for members of the Army Staff College, and whilst he was making his fourth flight in the He 162 the aircraft suddenly yawed, stalled and fell to the ground. Marks lost his life in the crash. The subsequent investigation attributed the accident to a loss of control following an upward roll that caused the wing to break up.

During the late summer of 1945, at least three He 162s were among some 50 captured German aircraft that were shipped to the United States under the control of Col Harold E Watson, an experienced test pilot with the USAAF's Air Technical Intelligence section. Arriving in the US in 1946, Gerhard Hanf's He 162A-2 Wk-Nr 120077 'Red 1' was overhauled at the USAAF experimental facility and test centre at Freeman Field, in Indiana. On 14 May 1946, the Technical Section of the Analysis Division, Intelligence (T-2) at Wright Field drafted the following report on the He 162;

'The Heinkel 162 employs as little critical material as possible. The most remarkable features of the design are the low span/length ratio, the mounting of the jet unit above the fuselage, the tricycle undercarriage, which retracts into

the fuselage, and the sharp dihedral of the tailplane. It is felt that many novel features in design and construction of this German jet fighter should be studied further relative to the possibility of incorporating the best features in future American types.'

The aircraft was eventually relocated to the University of Kansas at Lawrence, Kansas.

In early 1946, after negotiations with the British and the Americans, five He 162s were handed over to the French. Bernburg-built He 162A-1s Wk-Nr 310003 and Wk-Nr 310005, and Rostock-built He 162A-2s Wk-Nr 120015 'White 21', Wk-Nr 120093 and Wk-Nr 120223 'Yellow 1' were loaded onto rail wagons and moved under a British guard across the Rhine, despite damage to the bridges, to Andernach station on the French side of the river, where they arrived in March 1946. The Heinkels were subsequently transported to the *Societé Nationale de Construction Aéronautique du Centre* (SNCAC) at Boulogne-Billancourt for further evaluation.

It was decided to retain the three aforementioned A-2 machines for restoration to flying condition, while the two others – A-1s each equipped with MK 108s – would have their wings removed for further analysis and the cannon sent to the *Direction des Études et Fabrications d'Armement*. The three A-2s were then moved again, by road, to the airfield at Toussus-le-

A US Army soldier peers into the cockpit of He 162A-1 Wk-Nr 310027, which was built at Junkers' Bernburg plant and found by the Americans there in April 1945 in an almost factory-finished condition. Here, the cowlings have been opened to reveal the BMW 003 jet engine

With their engines and tail assemblies removed, these two He 162s have been loaded onto flatbed rail wagons at Leck for transporting to France. The fuselage to the left is Bernburg-built He 162A-1 Wk-Nr 310003 'Yellow 5', possibly the same aircraft flown by Leutnant Hans Berger of 3./JG 1 to Leck on 15 April 1945. The jet carries a colourful trio of JG 1's unit emblems representing, from left, the demon of I./JG 1, the Lion of Danzig of 3. *Staffel* and the winged '1' of JG 1 as a *Geschwader*. The airframe to the right is Wk-Nr 310005 'Red 7', the stem of the number just visible in the usual position aft of the cockpit. The rail wagon is marked 'France', but it would not arrive on French soil until March 1946

The BMW 003 jet engine of the all-blue He 162A-2 'No 3', formerly 'White 2' of 1./JG 1, blasts flame as it undergoes testing with the École de l'Air at Salon-de-Provence, in France, in February 1949

Noble, where over a period of one year they were carefully returned to flying condition – a remarkable achievement when it is considered that no manuals were available to the technicians. The BMW 003 engines, which had been removed from the fuselages for the rail journey from Germany, were sent to the *Compagnie Electro Mécanique* in Paris for overhaul.

It would not be until May the following year that the French actually flew their He 162s from Orléans-Bricy airfield with SNCAC factory pilots Abel Nicolle and Louis Bertrand at the controls. The aircraft had been reassigned French identification numbers, with Wk-Nr 120223 becoming 'No 1', Wk-Nr 120015 becoming 'No 2' and Wk-Nr 120093 becoming 'No 3'. Later testing of the *Volksjäger* by Lt Raphaël Lombaert on behalf of the *État-Major Général Air* (EMGA) resulted in an unfavourable report being produced in which sluggish acceleration, sensitivity to the slightest amount of slip, poor visibility and very short range were all highlighted.

During the summer of 1947, the three He 162s were moved by rail from Orléans-Bricy to the *Centre d'Études et d'Armement de Mulhouse* (CEAM) facility at Mont-de-Marsan, where they were thoroughly overhauled and repaired by CEAM mechanics with a specialisation in jet technology, civilian technicians from SNAC and a former engineer from BMW. By September the aircraft were ready for further flight trials, and on 25 October no fewer than 11 pilots flew the Heinkels on 20-minute high-speed familiarisation flights.

Testing continued into 1948, with the last recorded flight taking place on 23 July, when Capt Schlienger took off in clear weather with a very light southeasterly wind in Rostock-built Wk-Nr 120223 'No 1' from Mont-de-Marsan to conduct a demonstration flight for student officers. It was observed by the control tower that Schlienger's takeoff appeared somewhat slow, his aircraft lifting only a few metres off the ground with the undercarriage failing to retract. The tower immediately ordered the road at the end of the 2450 m runway to be kept closed to passing traffic, but after just one minute in the air above the surrounding pine trees, the Heinkel turned to port, with its wheels still down, stalled and crashed into the ground, exploding into flames with its BMW engine flung more than 60 m from the scene of impact.

It was concluded that Schlienger had possibly encountered difficulties with the electrics systems during takeoff. It was further decided that the He 162s were no longer of 'military value and of no practical interest'. The remaining machines were to be written off. However, in January 1949, 'No 2' was assigned as an instructional airframe to a mechanics' school in Rochefort-sur-Mer, where it remained until July 1952, on one occasion painted bright red while paraded through a nearby village for a local fete.

The Russians are believed to have acquired seven He 162s in various conditions, and at least two A-2s, coded '01' and '02' (one of them

He 162A-2 'Red 2' was one of up to seven such aircraft acquired by the Soviet Union and operated by the Flight Research Institute of the People's Commissariat for the Aircraft Industry. This machine is believed to have been built at Rostock and then moved directly to Russia, where it was flight-tested in 1946

believed to have been Wk-Nr 120020), were assembled at EHAG Rostock under Russian supervision. '02' flew for the first time under Soviet control on 8 May 1946 with Georgi M Shiyanov (a test pilot for the *Letno-Islyedovatel'skiy Institut* [LII] *Narodny Kommisariat Aviatsionoy Promishlinosti* – Flight Research Institute of the People's Commissariat for the Aircraft Industry) at the controls. Although the Russians viewed the Heinkel with some scepticism, Shiyanov, nevertheless, made two further flights five days later, as well as performing a demonstration flight before the Minister of Aircraft Production, Mikhail V Khrunishev, his deputy, Pyotr V Dementyev, and aircraft designers Aleksandr S Yakovlev and Artyom I Mikoyan on 11 July 1946. Another test pilot, A G Kochetkov, also made flights.

However, a subsequent LII report on the trials with the He 162 commented;

'According to the pilot, the aircraft has a low longitudinal stability margin – lateral stability is close to neutral. The aircraft is unpleasant to fly thanks to negative stability and the extra efficiency of the rudders. The long takeoff roll of 1350 m (with a flight weight 9.6 per cent below normal) indicates a very low takeoff lift coefficient. Further tests have ceased because the takeoff roll is too long.'

On 26 August 1946, the British freighter SS *Manchester Commerce* steamed out of Salford Docks in Manchester, bound for Montreal, Canada. On board were two He 162s, Wk-Nr 120076 (AM 59) and Wk-Nr 120086 (AM 62), destined for the Canadian government. The vessel berthed in Montreal on 9 September and the Heinkels would ultimately be deposited with the Canadian National Aeronautical Collection (CNAC) at Rockliffe, near Ottawa.

The remaining He 162s in England met with various fates, most of them ending up on the scrap heap.

In summary, this author is of the view that while it may be true that the pace and accomplishment of Luftwaffe operations with the He 162 did not, perhaps could not, mirror that of EHAG's spirited and tenacious attempts at development and production of the aircraft under Carl Francke, *Jagdgeschwader* 1 nevertheless proved, against all odds, that the technology and build-standard that EHAG had attained in such little time was, in contemporary parlance, 'fit for purpose' – just.

APPENDICES

APPENDIX 1

HEINKEL He 162A-1 (standard configuration)

Crew	1	
Engine	BMW 003 jet engine, model 003 E	
Ground level thrust, 30 second military rating	920 kg	
Ground level thrust, normal performance	800 kg	
Thrust performance at 800 km/h to 11,000 m (30 second boost)	332 kg	
Thrust performance at 800 km/h to 11,000 m (normal)	265 kg	
Actual fuel consumption at normal rating	1.61 kg/kg h	
Actual fuel consumption at 30 second rating	1.96 kg/kg h	

Span	7.2 m
Length	9.05 m
Height	2.6 m
Wing area	11.16 m^2
Wing loading	265 kg/m^2
Power loading	3.18 kg/kg
Aspect ratio	4.65
Empty weight	1663 kg
Auxiliary equipment	95 kg
Structural weight (including auxiliary equipment)	1758 kg
Weapons (2 x MK 108)	157 kg
Ammunition (2 x 50 rpg)	58 kg
Armour	57 kg
Crew	100 kg
Undercarriage, flaps and trims (with 61 kg trimming ballast)	983 kg

Engine with tank and cowling/fairing	680 kg
Fuel (excluding starter fuel)	675 kg
Takeoff weight	2805 kg
Taxiing and warming-up fuel	80 kg
Starting fuel	22 kg
Taxiing weight	2907 kg

Maximum speed at:

0 m	790 km/h normal	890 km/h (30 second boost)
6000 m	838 km/h	905 km/h
11,000 m	765 km/h	845 km/h

Full throttle endurance at:

0 m	30 mins	28 mins
6000 m	48 mins	46 mins
11,000 m	83 mins	81 mins

Full throttle range at:

0 m	390 km	370 km
6000 m	620 km	596 km
11,000 m	975 km	945 km

Climb Performance at:

0 m	19.2 m/sec	26.5 m/sec
6000 m	9.9 m/sec	16.0 m/sec
11,000 m	1.6 m/sec	5.8 m/sec
Takeoff distance	850 m	740 m
Takeoff distance to 15 m	980 m	810 m
Landing distance from 15 m	950 m	950 m
Landing speed	190 km/h	190 km/h

HEINKEL He 162A-1/A-2 (standard configuration – revised 4 October 1944)

Measurements

Aerodynamic area	11.16 m^2
Span	7.2 m
Length	9.05 m
Engine	BMW 003 A-1
Ground-level thrust	800 kg
Thrust at 800 km/h to 11 km	265 kg
Actual fuel consumption at this rating	1.61 kg/kg h

Weights

Weapons (2 x MK 108)	180 kg
Ammunition (2 x 50 rpg)	58 kg
Armour	70 kg
Equipment (without weapons and armour)	100 kg
Crew	100 kg
Military weight	508 kg
Undercarriage, flaps and trims	839 kg
Engine with tank	673 kg
Fuel	475 kg
Takeoff weight	2495 kg
Landing weight with 20 per cent fuel	2190 kg

Flight Performance

Maximum performance at 0 km	790 km/h
at 6 km	840 km/h
at 11 km	780 km/h
Calculated endurance at 0 km	20 mins
(Full power) at 6 km	33 mins
at 11 km	57 mins
Calculated range at 0 km	285 km
(Full power) at 6 km	430 km
at 11 km	660 km
Maximum range	700 km
Maxmimum climb with averafe flight weight at 0 km	21.5 m/sec
at 6 km	12.5 m/sec
at 11 km	3.5 m/sec
Climbing time from takeoff to 6 km	6.6 mins
to 11 km	20.0 mins
Takeoff distance without boost	850 m
Takeoff distance with 1000 kg boost thrust	320 m
Landing speed	165 km/h

Flight performance with 200 kg supplementary fuel

Calculated endurance at 0 km	30 mins	(Full power) at 13 km	1000 km
(Full power) at 11 km	85 mins	Takeoff distance without boost	800 m
Calculated range at 0 km	390 km	Takeoff distance with 1000 kg boost thrust	380 m

APPENDIX 2

ORGANISATION OF *JAGDGESCHWADER* 1 ON 1 MAY 1945

Geschwader Stab Oberst Herbert Ihlefeld

Adjutant	Oblt Wind
Ia	Hptm Reinbrecht
Ic	Hptm Liebrecht
NO	Hptm Kootz
Kfz.O	techn Ob Insp Mirbach
TO	Fl Ing Pfeiffer
zbV	Ltn Nitschke

I. Gruppe Major Werner Zober

Adjutant	Oblt Stärk
Ia	Oblt Vogt
TO	Fl O Ing Hansen
WO	W Insp Weigelt
Meteor	Reg Rat Lopsien
NO	Ltn Suchy
Kfz.Ot	Insp Heese
IVa	Stabsint Siegfried
IVb	Stabsarzt Dr Seebach

Stabskompanie I./JG 1

Chef	Hptm Hans Bleser
zbV	Ltn Hans Bittern
Spies	Hptfw Heinz Irmisch
Plus	64 *Unteroffiziere* and 125 men

1. Staffel

possibly Ltn Rudolf Schmitt (flying)

Hptm Heinz Künnecke (non-flying)

Technical Officer   Ltn Dörr

Pilots

Ltn Dolderer

Ltn Erlat

Ltn Schröder

Fw Gudrath

Fw Horny

Fw Steeb

Uffz von Alvensleben

Uffz Dosch

Uffz Nieswohl

Uffz Riehl

2. Staffel

possibly Ltn Gerhard Hanf and Oblt W Wollenweber (flying)

Hptm Wolfgang Ludewig (non-flying)

Technical Officer   Ltn Heinen

Pilots

Ltn Feldt

Ltn Deppe

Ltn Rechenberg

Ltn Rodatz

Ltn Hofmann

Ltn Langer

Fw Schücking

Fw Gold

Fw Gehrlein

Fw Kreutz

Fw Schlösser

Uffz Cranz

Uffz Fenger

Uffz Augner

Uffz Widnemann

Uffz Harder

3. Staffel

possibly Ltn Hans Berger and Oblt W Wollenweber (flying)

Oblt Karl-Emil Demuth (possibly non-flying)

Technical Officer   Oblt Krebs

Pilots

Ltn Hanf

Ltn Stenschke

Ltn Stiemer

Ltn Köttgen

Ltn Kriete

Ltn Friese

Ltn Lange

Ltn Klein

Fhr Köhler

Fw Bartzen

Uffz Rieder

Uffz Brüne

Uffz Brandt

Uffz Schaumburg

Uffz Bauch

II. (Sammel) Gruppe Hauptmann Rahe (non flying)

Adjutant

Oblt Beugler

4. Staffel

Hptm Bernd Gallowitsch (non-flying)

possibly Ltn 'Schmidt' (Schmitt?)

Fl.Oberstabsing Neuner

Fl.Stabsing Müller

Tech.Oberinsp Talinski

Tech.Oberinsp Müller

Fl.Ing Radomicki

5. Staffel

Hptm Bergholz (non-flying)

zbV Oblt Pilz

6. Staffel

Oblt Zipprecht (non-flying)

zbV Ltn Werth

COLOUR PLATES

1
He 162 V1 Wk-Nr 200001 'VI+IA', Vienna-Schwechat, December 1944
The He 162 prototype was completed in early December 1944 and finished in overall RLM 02, with the only other marking being the *Werknummer* painted in black on the lower part of the fin. The fuselage *Balkenkreuz* was of an early style. The aircraft was destroyed when it crashed on its second flight on 6 December while being flown by Flugkapitän Dipl-Ing Gotthold Peter.

2
He 162A-1 Wk-Nr 310001, Bernburg, February 1945
The first aircraft to be delivered by Junkers at Bernburg had its fuselage painted in RLM 82/76. The colour demarcation line was bold and ran roughly along the centreline of the fuselage. The engine unit was in a brown colour, probably RLM 81, with the rear panel in black. 'Lippisch ears' were absent on this early machine. The aircraft was flown for the first time by Junkers test pilot Hermann Steckhan on 15 February 1945.

3
He 162 M20 Wk-Nr 220003 'VI+IM', Lechfeld, March 1945
This was the third pre-production series aircraft. The fuselage was painted in RLM 76/82, with the rear fuselage cone having the appearance of a natural metal finish – the camouflage was applied to the upper side only. The BMW 003 engine cowling and covering was painted in RLM 81, with the wing uppersurfaces finished in RLM 81/82. This aeroplane made its first flight with Gerhard Gleuwitz at the controls on 10 February 1945.

4
He 162S of the *Reichsegelflugschule*, Trebbin, March 1945
The only known prototype of the two-seat glider version of the He 162 was the 'S' (for '*Spatz*' – Sparrow). The fuselage was finished in RLM 82/76, with the fins, which were squarer and smaller than the powered production version, mottled in RLM 82. The *Balkenkreuz* was of an early style.

5
He 162 M23 (A-06) Wk-Nr 220006 'VI+IP', Heidfeld, March 1945
This aircraft was finished in RLM 02 overall, with the exception of the rear panel of the engine unit in RLM 81. The *Werknummer* 220006 was painted on both the top and bottom of the fins, whilst the aircraft's prototype number appeared in black beneath the forward canopy. It was first flown by Gerhard Gleuwitz on 19 March 1945.

6
He 162A-2 Wk-Nr 120072 'Yellow 3' of 3./JG 1, Ludwigslust, April 1945
The upper half of the fuselage was finished in RLM 82 along with the tail fins, while the engine unit was in RLM 81, with the forward intake ring in RLM 02 and the rear section in black. The *Werknummer* was in white, as was the nose cone, which may have been a replacement unit. The emblem of 3./JG 1 was carried just below the canopy.

7
He 162A-1 Wk-Nr 120016(?) 'White 21' of 1./JG 1, Ludwigslust, April 1945
'White 21' was finished in a scheme of RLM 82/76, but the 82 was applied only to the uppermost surfaces. The bulk of the fuselage was left in plain 76. The tip of the nose was adorned in the national military colours of red, white and black, along with a single red arrow on either side. The fins were 82 overall, with the *Werknummer* in white. The front engine unit panel was in RLM 81. The *Werknummer* of this aircraft is uncertain.

8
He 162A-2 Wk-Nr 120077 'Red 1' of 2./JG 1, Leck, April 1945
Flown by Leutnant Gerhard Hanf, this machine featured a scheme typical of EHAG Rostock mid-production aircraft, although the tail fins were in RLM 76 and the engine unit was in RLM 81, the rear section being in black. The nose was adorned on both sides with JG 1's occasional red arrow markings as well as the emblem of III./JG 77, Hanf's previous unit. A personal motto '*Nervenklau*' ('Nerve Jangler') was also applied just below the cockpit, but probably after the war.

9
He 162A-2 possibly Wk-Nr 120013 'White 1' of 1./JG 1, Leck, May 1945
This was the aircraft that Leutnant Rudolf Schmitt was flying when he fired at an RAF Tempest V fighter over Husum on 4 May 1945. The fuselage was finished almost entirely in RLM 76, with just a small area of RLM 82 between the engine and the cockpit. The tail fins were in RLM 81 and the wings in RLM 70 overall. The engine unit was in RLM 02/70 and black and the diving eagle emblem of 1./JG 1 was aft of the tactical '1' below the cockpit.

10
He 162A-1 possibly Wk-Nr 310078 'White 5' of 1./JG 1, probably Leck, May 1945
There is some uncertainty as to which pilot(s) flew this aircraft and where from, but it was finished in RLM 82/76. The uppersurfaces of the wings were painted in RLM 81/82 and the tail fins were in different colours, with the left side in 76 and the right side in 82. Additionally, they each carried differing *Hakenkreuze*, suggesting one unit was a replacement at some stage. The diving eagle emblem of 1./JG 1 was applied only to the port side of the aircraft.

11
He 162A-2 Wk-Nr 120067 'White 4' of 1./JG 1, Leck, May 1945
'White 4' was finished in RLM 82/76, with a demarcation running along the fuselage centre line. The aircraft's tactical number was aft of the cockpit and the emblem of 1. *Staffel* was only applied to the left side of the aircraft below the cockpit, with the red arrows of JG 1 on both sides. The *Balkenkreuz* was a plain black outline. The gun ports were in black. Generally, the aircraft had a worn look, and the right side tail fin was a replacement part in RLM 76 with edges in 81.

12
He 162A-2 Wk-Nr 120074 'Yellow 11' of I./JG 1, Leck, May 1945

The distinctive aircraft of Oberleutnant Karl-Emil Demuth as seen at Leck was finished in RLM 82/76 with a low demarcation line. The engine unit was in RLM 81, the rear section being in black and the intake ring in 02. The nose had red, white and black rings and the red *Geschwader* arrows, behind which was I. *Gruppe's* 'Devil in the Clouds' emblem. The tactical number '11' was aft of the cockpit, and also featured a small figure '20' in white, the meaning of which is not known. The right side fin was decorated with 16 victory markings at the top and the *Werknummer* at the bottom.

13
He 162A-2 Wk-Nr 120230 'White 23' of *Stab* JG 1, Leck, May 1945

Some sources state that this aircraft was assigned to the *Geschwaderkommodore* of JG 1, Oberst Herbert Ihlefeld, although as far as is known Ihlefeld never flew it operationally. The fuselage was finished in RLM 82/76, the upper wings in RLM 81/82 and the fin and rudder in RLM 76. The aircraft was among those captured at Leck.

14
He 162A-2 Wk-Nr 120098, recoded VH513/AM 67, RAE Farnborough, September 1945 (possibly formerly 'White 2' of JG 1 at Leck)

The aircraft was finished in RLM 82/76, with the engine unit in

RLM 81 and the forward intake ring in 02. The nose had JG 1's red arrow markings on both sides, as well as a red ring around the entire nose immediately in front of the cockpit. When the fighter was taken over by the British, the German wing and fuselage crosses were replaced by RAF roundels and an RAF tail fin marking was also applied.

15
He 162A-2 'Red 01', LII, Moscow, spring 1946

The Russians are known to have painted their first two Heinkels in an overall silver-grey, with the exception of the engine intake ring which was in red and the rear of the engine unit in black. The Soviet star was applied to the fuselage and tail fins, and the emblem of the *Letno-Islyedovatel'skiy Institut Narodny Kommisariat Aviatsionoy Promishlinosti* (Flight Research Institute of the People's Commissariat for the Aircraft Industry) was carried on the right-side tail fin only.

16
He 162A-2 No 2, SNCAC, Orléans-Bricy, 1947 (formerly 'White 21' of 1./JG 1)

JG 1's 'White 21' was repainted overall in French 'cockade blue' after its transfer to the *École de l'Air* in Salon de Provence, with the exception of the engine intake ring which remained in the German RLM 02 and the rear of the engine unit which was in white. The aeroplane was later flight-tested by the *Societé Nationale de Construction Aéronautique du Centre* at Orléans-Bricy airfield.

SOURCES AND BIBLIOGRAPHY

UNPUBLISHED MATERIAL

Ernst Heinkel Aktiengesellschaft (EHAG) – file of papers comprising reports, letters, file notes, cables and teleprint messages mainly despatched from EHAG from late 1944 to May 1945

Various *Flugbuch*

UK National Archives, Kew (Selected Documents)

AIR40/164 Günter, S and Hohbach *History and Experiences of He 162 and He 162 Report No. 2 Performances with Jumo-004 (Heinkel Report)*, Translation No. F-TS-672-RE, Headquarters Air Materiel Command, Wright Field, Dayton, Ohio, October 1946

AIR40/164 *Interim Report No. 1 on the German Jet Fighter Heinkel 162*, Interim Report No F-IM -1113A-ND, HQ, Air Materiel Command, 14 May 1946

AIR40/2421: ADI(K) Report No 185/1945 *Heinkel – Wien/ Schwechat and Ludwigslust*, July 1945

Imperial War Museum, London and Duxford (Selected Documents)

GDC/18/205 EHAG Aktenvermerk Nr 5/44, *162 Konstruktionbespechung*, 7.10.44

GDC/18 64, EHAG Wien, *Prüfmappe Flugzeug 162*, 1.2.45

CIOS: '*Jet-Fighter Heinkel 162 (Volksjäger)*'. Evaluation Report 166a, 7 July 1945

Miscellaneous Allied Document (Selected Documents)

Air P/W Interrogation Unit, Main Headquarters Second TAF *Trends of Development in the GAF – Part IV – The Story of the 8-162*, AP/WIU (2nd TAF) 87/1945, 12.7.1945

ADI(K) Report No 340/1945, *Arguments for and against the Volksjäger*, 26 June 1945

APWIU (2nd Air Disarmament Wing) 63/1945, *A View on the Volksjäger He 162*, 14 June 1945

Farren Mission to Germany: *He. 162 – An Achievement in Rapid Aircraft Dovclopment and Manufacture* (undated report)

Visit to select German aeroplanes of Category 1 May 29th-June 3rd, 1945, G M Buxton, Central Fighter Establishment, CFE/S.960/Eng., 8 June 1945

Enemy Aircraft Flight, Central Fighter Establishment: *Report of work on German orthodox and jet aircraft in Germany from 18.5.45 to 13.6.45*, Flt Lt R T H Collis, OC, EA Flight, EAF/S.50/AIR, 13 June 1945

German Documents (EXCL. EHAG) (Selected Documents)

Projekt Volksjäger – Stellungnahme zum Projekt Volksjäger von Dr. Vogt (Blohm & Voss) unter Berücksichtigung des Entwurfs Heinkel He 162 (undated)

Kommando der Erprobungsstellen Rechlin, 430/45 8-161 – *Besprechung am 11.2.1945 in Wien-Schwechat*, (13.2.1945)

PUBLISHED ARTICLES

Brown, CBE, DSC, AFC, RN, Captain Eric, *Mastering Heinkel's Minimus, Air Enthusiast*, June 1972

Chapman, A R '*Abschuß mit He 162 – JA oder NEIN?*', *Flugzeug* 1/89

Couderchon, Philippe, *The Salamander in France* (Parts 1 & 2), *Aeroplane*, April & May 2006

Griehl, Manfred, *Heinkels Verschleißjäger – Die Entwicklung der He 162 (Teil 1), Flugzeug* 5/95

Hanf, Gerhard, '*Ich flog die He 162 'Nervenklau*'', *Jägerblatt* Nr 4/XL, September/Oktober 1992

Heinkel – Die Zeitschrift dr Heinkel-Werke, Heft 1, 1 Dezember 1962

Heinkel 162 – JG 1, Luftwaffe Verband, Issue Number 12, October 1997

Lächler, Hans, '*Die letzten Wochen des 'Volksjägers',* Modell Magazin* 7/84

SELECTED PUBLISHED BOOKS

Beauvais, Heinrich, Kössler, Karl, Mayer, Max and Regel, Christoph, *German Secret Flight Test Centres to 1945*, Midland Publishing, Hinckley, 2002

Brown, Captain Eric 'Winkle', *Wings on my Sleeve*, Weidenfeld & Nicolson, London, 2006

Brütting, Georg, *Das Buch der deutschen Fluggeschichte: Band 3*, Drei Brunnen Verlag, Stuttgart, 1979

Butler, Phil, *War Prizes – An Illustrated Survey of German, Italian and Japanese Aircraft Brought to Allied Countries during and after the Second World War*, Midland Counties Publications, Leicester, 1994

Dennis, Richard, *Royal Aircraft Establishment at War*, Tutor Publications, Dorchester, 2008

Geust, Carl-Fredrik, *Under the Red Star – Luftwaffe Aircraft in the Soviet Air Force*, Airlife, Shrewsbury, 1993

Geust, C F and Petrov, G, *Red Stars Vol 2 – German Aircraft in the Soviet Union*, Apali Oy, Tampere, 1998

Forsyth, Robert, *Heinkel He 162 – From Drawing Board to Destruction – the Volksjäger*, Classic Publications, Hersham, 2008

Hiller, Dr Alfred, *Heinkel He 162 'Volksjäger' – Entwicklung – Produktion – Einsatz*, Verlag Hiller, Wien, 1984

Kay, Antony L, *German Jet Engine and Gas Turbine Development 1930-1945*, Airlife Publishing, Shrewsbury, 2002

Koos, Volker, *Heinkel Raketen- und Strahlflugzeuge*, Aviatic Verlag, Oberhaching, 2008

Mombeek, Eric, *Defending the Reich: The History of Jagdgeschwader 1 'Oesau'*, JAC Publications, Norwich, 1992

Mombeek, Eric, *Reichsverteidigung – Die Geschichte des Jagdgeschwaders 1 'Oesau'*, Eric Mombeek, 1993

Mombeek, Eric, *Defenders of the Reich – Jagdgeschwader 1 – Volume Three 1944-1945*, Classic Publications, Hersham, 2003

Müller, Peter, *Heinkel He 162 'Volksjäger' – Last-Ditch Effort by the Luftwaffe*, History Facts, Andelfingen, 2006

Obermaier, Ernst, *Die Ritterkreuzträger der Luftwaffe 1939-1945 – Band I Jagdflieger*, Verlag Dieter Hoffmann, Mainz, 1966

Prien, Jochen and Rodeike, Peter, *Jagdgeschwader 1 und 11 – Teil 3 1944-1945*, Eutin, undated

Smith, J Richard and Creek, Eddie J, *Jet Planes of the Third Reich*, Monogram Aviation Publications, Boylston, 1982

Smith, J Richard and Creek, Eddie J, *Volksjäger*, Monogram Close-Up 11, Monogram Aviation Publications, Boylston, 1986

Smith, J Richard and Creek, Eddie J, *Me 262 Volume One*, Classic Publications, Burgess Hill, 1997

Smith, J Richard and Creek, Eddie J, *Me 262 Volume Two,* Classic Publications, Burgess Hill, 1998

Wiesinger, Günter and Schroeder, Walter, *Die Österreichischen Ritterkreuzträger in der Luftwaffe 1939-45*, H Weishaupt Verlag, Graz, 1986

Wollenweber, Wolfgang, *Thunder over the Reich – Flying the Luftwaffe's He 162 Jet Fighter*, Hikoki Publications/Crecy Publishing, Manchester, 2014

INDEX